THEN THE CURTAIN OPENED

THEN THE CURTAIN OPENED

CHRISTIAN MINISTRY IN EASTERN EUROPE

CLIVE DOUBLEDAY

WITH EMMA WATKINS

CROSSWAY BOOKS

CROSSWAY BOOKS
38 De Montfort Street, Leicester LE1 7GP, England

First published 1998

British Library Cataloguing in Publication Data
A catalogue record for this book is available from the British Library.

ISBN 1–85684–160–X

Set in Franklin Gothic and Garamond

Typeset in Great Britain by Parker Typesetting Service, Leicester
Printed in Great Britain by The Guernsey Press, Guernsey, Channel Islands

To my lovely wife Ruth
without whose love and continued support
this book would not have been written

CONTENTS

FOREWORD

The end of the Cold War has brought about fundamental changes in Eastern and Western Europe. I believe that these changes have come about because Christians put their roots down in God and paid the price for our liberty.

Recently I received the Religious Liberties Award from the World Evangelization Fellowship for my work on behalf of suffering and persecuted believers over the last forty years. In my acceptance speech I told the assembled body that I could not have done this work alone. I received the Award on behalf of those many teams of Christians who worked with me, shoulder to shoulder, in serving the suffering church. Thank you, Clive and Ruth, for being among those faithful Christians.

Nothing pleases me more than to read of those who follow in the footsteps of earlier pioneering missionaries, allowing God to pour his life through them in the former strongholds of Communism. But it does not stop there. The body of Christ living under the powerful domination of Islam has a special focus for me in these days. We are reminded in this book about Islam and new cults sweeping across our world, including Eastern Europe. Will any of us, I wonder, pay the price for someone else's freedom?

This is not just another book. Read it and let God speak to you.

Brother Andrew

PREFACE

On Christmas Day 1963, an eight-year-old boy was given an old teak-coloured radio. He was fascinated. He heard broadcasts from all over the world, and developed a special interest in Russia, Romania and East Germany (as it then was). He wrote to radio stations behind the Iron Curtain, and gradually built up a wide knowledge of mysterious and exotic places – Bucharest, Budapest, Moscow, Berlin, Sofia . . .

I was that small boy. I have since been privileged to visit many of those places, so that mere names have become real locations, populated, above all, with real people, now friends.

I gave my life to Christ in 1977, and after many jobs, much travelling and marriage to Ruth, I knew that God was calling me to the Christian ministry.

In 1986 our daughter Emily was born, and in 1987 we moved to London so that I could undertake a four-year degree course in theology at Spurgeon's College as part of my Baptist ministerial training. Throughout this period, our interest in and concern for Christians in Eastern Europe never waned. In fact, on completion of my student days at Spurgeon's, I was offered a post on the staff as Director of Communications, and part of my responsibility was to oversee and develop the Overseas Bursary Fund which was being used to support students from Russia, Romania, Bulgaria and Albania. I was also able to lead a number of special missions to these East European countries, details of which are recorded in this book.

After the collapse of Communism in 1989, the growth of evangelical Christianity in Eastern Europe has raced ahead, and new churches, theological seminaries, Christian radio stations and Christian social projects have been established throughout Central and Eastern Europe. I have written this book to highlight some of these developments, as well as to encourage Christians in the West to continue to pray, support and even visit these countries, so that the church there may be edified and encouraged in their work of spreading the good news of the gospel.

This book is a testimony to the faithfulness of many Christians who have served God, often in the face of persecution and hardship, in many small villages, towns and large cities behind the Iron Curtain. Without the help and prayerful support of many Christians in the West, too, the missions and aid convoys to our needy brothers and sisters in the East would not have been possible.

Many Christians have encouraged me to write the book, having heard me speak about the needs of Eastern Europe in churches, colleges, homes and meetings throughout the UK. I am grateful to Derek Wood, Senior Editor of Crossway Books, for his diligence, encouragement and perseverance, which ensured that the book became a reality; and to Malcolm Walker of the Keston Institute in Oxford, who assisted me in my research. I am honoured that Brother Andrew has written the foreword, and thank God for his faithful ministry with Open Doors over many decades. I am also grateful to David Culwick, Chief Executive of Spurgeon's Child Care, and to Michael Rowe, Russian translator, researcher, and author of *Russian Resurrection*, for their warm commendations.

My wife Ruth and our two children, Emily and Timothy, supported me and encouraged me to get these stories into print. My church in Petts Wood has offered unstinting support, love and encouragement. Beryl Pratt, my secretary, typed several drafts of the book; her patience and persistence have been a great encouragement to me. Emma Watkins has helped to mould the book into its present form, using her experience of Eastern Europe and her journalistic expertise. To her I am extremely grateful.

I trust the book will be a blessing and a challenge to all who read it.

Clive Doubleday

1

TO RUSSIA WITH
LOVE, 1984

Russia is the world's largest country, extending across eleven time zones between the Baltic Sea and the Pacific Ocean. From the time of its foundation in the eighth century until the fall of Communism in 1991, it was ruled by autocrats, many of whom were tyrants. The tsarist empire collapsed in 1917, when the Bolshevik Revolution introduced Communist rule. Russia dominated the USSR from its conception in 1922. Its Communist leaders exploited both the ordinary Russian people and the many ethnic groups and client satellite states which it either seized or controlled. The resentment of those who had been oppressed hastened the dismemberment of the USSR once central control in Moscow was weakened. Multi-party democracy was instituted in 1990, but a failed coup by Communist hard-liners in August 1991 led to the subsequent banning of the Communist Party. The battle between the reformist democrats, supported by Boris Yeltsin, and the ex-Communist leadership supported by the Prime Minister, Viktor Chernomyrdin, led, by 1993, to a stalemate, which prevented constitutional reform, delayed economic reforms and hastened the collapse of central government.

For seventy years, the overt policy of the Communist Party was the elimination of religious 'superstition'. Atheism was promoted, and all open expressions of faith were forbidden. All religions were vigorously repressed, restricted, persecuted, subverted or manipulated to further Communist goals. Millions died or were imprisoned

for their faith, and thousands of churches destroyed. Under the post-Communist government, religious freedom is constitutionally guaranteed, although a Bill has passed repeatedly between Parliament and President Yeltsin, threatening to restrict the liberty of some non-Orthodox groups (see page 135).
(Source: *Operation World*)

Bibles to Leningrad

In the summer of 1984, my wife Ruth and I were given the opportunity to deliver Bibles into the Soviet Union for Open Doors. The Bibles were hidden in our camper van at the secluded Open Doors base in Holland, and only I was shown where, so that if Ruth were questioned, she would not have a clue what to say. During the long drive to Leningrad we memorized a series of dates, times and places so that we would know when and where to hand over the Bibles. If the first contact did not materialize, we had to go to a different street the next day. If that contact failed to show up also, then another place had been designated for the pick-up, and so on. Before we entered the Soviet Union, we burned the information that we had now learned by heart.

On arrival at the desolate checkpoint on the Soviet border, we were somewhat surprised to discover that there were only three cars entering the country. We watched in amazement as nine guards, complete with sniffer dogs, took apart a German Mercedes. We prayed that they would be less industrious when it came to our turn. The stocky officer in charge had a face like flint, hard and grey. She wore a small, pointed army cap and looked as if she had just stepped out of a Colditz film.

When the guards finally came to us, we had to erect our trailer tent and show them inside. They looked under the trailer tent, under the car, in our suitcases and in the engine. As they climbed into the trailer tent, their heads were literally inches from the roof inside which the Bibles were hidden.

The stern-looking officer saw Ruth knitting a baby jacket for some friends of ours, and wrongly assumed that she was pregnant. She immediately ordered the rest of the guards to stop searching our vehicle and let us go. Within minutes we had passed through the checkpoint and were on the road into Russia.

The first thing we noticed was that there were hardly any cars anywhere. We were given permission to drive on one road only, the Intourist road. Every twenty miles there was a checkpoint where papers were inspected. Travellers were timed from one checkpoint to the next, and, if they did not arrive on time, a search party was sent looking for them. As we drove along, we remembered that Christians would be looking out for our car (which was a conspicuous bright yellow), and notifying others that we had entered the country as scheduled. We wondered whether the little girls picking flowers, or the farmers with their sheep and cows, or the old ladies selling fruit by the side of the road, were part of this internal network of Christians.

Campsite or concentration camp?

At one point we took a wrong turning and ended up in the market square of a little town. Being the only car visible, we attracted attention. The townspeople were quite friendly, but were extremely anxious to point us back on to the Intourist road for fear that the police would come and interrogate them on account of our simple navigational error. We found our way back on to the correct road and continued on towards our campsite on the edge of Leningrad.

The campsite looked more like a concentration camp. A high fence topped with barbed wire surrounded the whole site, which was patrolled by guard dogs and guards, making the rounds with their sub-machine guns several times a day. We had to hand over our passports as we checked in to make sure that we did not leave without paying the 30p a night it cost to camp there.

Half of the camp consisted of little apex wooden houses and the other half of tents and caravans. The toilets and showers were extremely basic, but a walk around the site revealed a shop and a hotel. The people around the place were friendly.

We ate that night in the hotel's restaurant, a massive ballroom with great colonnades of pillars. There were about a dozen waiters, but only six guests, in a room which looked fit to be the setting for state banquets.

The following day we headed into the city to try to find our contact points. As we wandered around we noticed that nobody would actually look at us as they passed. Fraternizing with westerners was an offence in Russia in those days.

The shops were dull, dark and empty, the roads and pavements were full of huge potholes, and trams clanked along the street noisily. Nevertheless, Leningrad – now renamed St Petersburg – is an intriguing city. Its vistas of elegant buildings across the wide Neva river recall Paris, Amsterdam, Venice or Berlin. But its beauty is all is own, happily little harmed by Stalinist reconstruction. Even the colourful domes of Moscow are a rarity in this more severe, geometrical city, whose grey stone and harsh northern light are illuminated by occasional splashes of colour – the green and gold of the Winter Palace, the red beside the Anichkov Bridge, the blue of Smolny Cathedral.

St Petersburg has many claims to fame. The great Russian ballet dancer Nijinsky was trained here, and the nineteenth-century flowering of Russian music was centred here around composers such as Tchaikovsky and Rimsky-Korsakov. The great Russian poet, Pushkin, was educated in Leningrad. Dostoevsky set his novel *Crime and Punishment* here.

In the Second World War, the city suffered terribly. Hitler besieged it from 8 September 1941 to 27 January 1944, and during that period it is estimated that three-quarters of a million people died from shelling, starvation and disease. (The USA and the UK lost about the same number between them during the whole length of the war.) After the war, Leningrad was reborn, and became the Soviet Union's biggest port and second-largest industrial centre.

Follow that man!

After spending several hours touring the city and getting our bearings, we made our way to our first point of contact, hoping and praying that the person would be there. Our instructions were to enter a certain Metro station at two o'clock in the afternoon. While on the platform we were to look for someone who would be carrying a western bag.

At two o'clock we were in position and looked around inconspicuously to see if anyone resembled our contact. A few minutes later a train pulled into the station and off stepped a six-foot-tall man wearing a raincoat. He was carrying 'our' bag. Our instructions were not to make contact with him, but simply to follow him until he made contact with us. He boarded a train going in the opposite direction, and we only just managed to get on, keeping our eyes fixed firmly on him. After about ten minutes and five stops later, he got off. We followed at a distance of about thirty yards along a narrow street.

After a while, Ruth whispered to me that somebody was following us. We now faced a dilemma. We tried to keep our eyes on the man in front and simultaneously look back to see who was following us. On the next street, I saw the man. We crossed the road. He crossed the road. We stopped at a bridge. He stopped at the bridge. We were not sure whether he was from the KGB and waiting to arrest us and our contact, who went into a park.

As we followed him in, a wasp stung Ruth's hand and she gave out a yell, which caused a number of people to glance in our direction. While we bound her hand up, the man who was following us passed us by and headed towards our contact, who was talking with another man at an entrance booth. We didn't know if we should shout the contact a warning, but before we could, the man following us had reached him and seemed to know him. They suddenly disappeared into a sunken garden. We followed and found them there waiting to greet us. This situation perplexed us somewhat, but we discovered that the man following us was also a Christian, who was working in partnership with our contact to ensure that nobody was following him.

We were instructed to give the code so that they knew who we were. One of the Russian men said his half of the code wrongly, which left us in some doubt. But he urged us to respond, and when we did, he asked us how many Bibles we had. I had no idea, but he pressed me; so I gave an estimate of about a hundred, at which he seemed disappointed. I thought he was being ungrateful. Only time would tell how many Bibles there were in our camper van.

He then took us to the handover spot where we were due to present him with the Bibles the following night. We walked for miles, until we reached the first drop point by a river where the street lamps did not work. He explained to us how the handover would be made, and then took us on to four more locations, any of which could be used if it turned out that the street lights in the other places had been fixed.

Back at our campsite, we spent the rest of the day trying to work out whether it was a set-up or a genuine contact, as we had been told not to hand over the Bibles unless the contact got the code perfectly right. We toiled with this decision all afternoon, but remembered some verses from Proverbs which seemed remarkably apt and which encouraged us to go forward:

> Have no fear of sudden disaster
>   or of the ruin that overtakes the wicked,
> for the LORD will be your confidence
>   and will keep your foot from being snared.
>
> Do not withhold good from those who deserve it,
>   when it is in your power to act.
> Do not say to your neighbour,
>   'Come back later; I'll give it tomorrow' –
> when you now have it with you.
>
>   (3: 25–28)

The next day we decided to leave the campsite early as if for an evening's entertainment, to avoid suspicion. Before we left we decided to extricate the Bibles from their hiding-place. Inside the secret compartment was a long canvas wallet which I pulled out, like a magician pulling an endless handkerchief out of his top hat. The wallet was full of pockets, and in each pocket were Russian New Testaments. I pulled and pulled and pulled, and the Bibles kept coming out. There were literally hundreds of them.

As I was getting some holdalls out of the car to put them in, the security guards came round on their motorbikes. They tootled round the camp with their guns, ensuring that everything was in order. I just smiled at them and waved. They waved back. But I was praying and sweating.

The Red Sea opens

The first difficulty was getting out of the campsite. Usually the guards were very swift at opening the red and white barrier, but on this occasion they stopped us to check our details. The next challenge, a hundred yards down the road, was the main checkpoint at the city limits, with the Russian police. To our great relief and by the grace of God, we were waved through. We then had twenty-two sets of traffic lights to go through. We had observed the day before that at each set of traffic lights there was an armed policeman who, if he rested his white baton on your bonnet, would make you get out, show him your authorization papers, open your boot and show him anything you were carrying. As we drove along we prayed incessantly that God would open up the way for us to reach our destination. Every set of lights was on green. It felt as if God had parted the Red Sea for us as we drove our precious cargo into the heart of the city to meet our Russian Christian contacts.

As we drove through the city, people tried to wave us down, as our yellow car was mistaken for a taxi. We simply smiled and waved back. We parked at the Hotel Continental, the best hotel in the city and the safest place to leave our western vehicle. We still had over two hours before we needed to be at the drop point, so we decided to go to the cinema. We found one where *The Hound of the Baskervilles* was showing, and settled into our seats.

A few minutes later, half a dozen police came and sat right in front of us. Just before the film started, about twenty Russian soldiers came and sat behind us. Sandwiched between the police and these soldiers, we engrossed ourselves in the film until the alarm clock I had brought with us beeped in the dark. Fortunately, the music on the film got louder at that point, but I sat on the clock anyway to muffle the noise. (It has never been the same since!) We got up to leave, but were accosted by an enthusiastic usher who expressed concern that we were wasting our money by leaving early. The only way we could convince him that we wanted to go was by indicating that Ruth needed some air. The doors were unbolted (we had been locked in) and we were allowed out, though not without a display of indignation at us westerners who had paid good money (about 10p each) to see a film and walked out before it was finished.

The five-minute kiss

Though we had been told by our contact not to arrive a minute sooner or later than expected, we reached the drop point fifteen minutes early and parked a distance away. As we wandered about looking at the river, a police car pulled up and parked right behind our car, just feet away from the thousand Bibles in our boot. The policeman took out binoculars and pointed them in our direction. To look inconspicuous, I grabbed hold of Ruth and started kissing and cuddling her, as any young couple would do. As we kissed, I kept asking Ruth whether they were still watching us, but after five minutes they had had enough, and went away.

At exactly the appointed hour we were at the drop point. The street lights had not been fixed. We identified the right car and backed up to it boot to boot, even though we were still in some doubt whether this was a genuine contact. Just as I was about to get out of the car, an ambulance came hurtling round the corner at tremendous speed with bells ringing and lights flashing. Both our hearts stopped with fear.

I got out of the car and quickly lifted the Bibles from my boot into theirs. They blessed us and thanked us for coming, and we drove away. After months of planning, praying, and driving 1,500 miles through six countries, we had handed over our precious cargo in just sixty seconds.

At the corner of the street, a young couple in their late teens, obviously young Christians, were on the lookout. We smiled and briefly waved as we drove off, realizing what a tremendous sacrifice it was that these young people were willing to make simply to get hold of the Word of God. If they had been arrested they would probably have been transported to Siberia, whereas we would just have been kicked out of the country. Our admiration for them was immense. We understood from our contacts in Holland that these Bibles would be transported throughout the country and that some would reach as far as the Ural mountains some two thousand miles further east.

The next day we would have been happy to leave Leningrad, but our visa insisted that we stay five days and spend a minimum of twenty roubles a day. We spent a day at the tsars' Winter Palace in the river, where the fountains, gardens and palace itself were stunning. The building is a rococo profusion of columns, windows and recesses topped with larger-than-lifesize statues. The tsars had lived in this great luxury while the serfs, 90% of the population, struggled to keep going. The palace is now the biggest part of the Hermitage art museum. Other impressive buildings in the city include the Admiralty and St Isaac's Cathedral, yet it is the Hermitage which attracts the largest number of foreign visitors. This massive building has 1,057 rooms and 117 staircases.

In our wanderings around the city, we tried to find the Baptist church, but without success. It was sad to see that a lot of church buildings had been converted into factories or museums, and I wondered then whether they would ever again echo to the sound of men and women singing praises to God.

This first journey in Eastern Europe taught Ruth and me a great lesson. We witnessed Christian commitment as we had never seen it before. These young Christians in Russia were literally willing to lose their life for their faith so that others could have the Word of God and come to know Jesus Christ as their Lord and Saviour.

The ethics of smuggling

Some Christians believe that Christians should not smuggle Bibles, since to do so is to defy the authorities of the countries entered. They often cite Romans 13:1–7, which encourages us to submit to the ruling authorities, who, Paul says, 'hold no terror for those who do right, but for those who do wrong'. Here, however, Paul is describing the proper, ideal function of rulers. When those rulers overstep that function, Christians are to obey God rather than human beings, as Peter and the other apostles declared when forbidden to teach in the name of Jesus: 'Judge for yourselves whether it is right in God's sight to obey you rather than God' (Acts 4:19); 'We must obey God rather than men!' (Acts 5:29).

I believe no-one should be prevented by any government, political party or anti-Christian regime from having access to the Word of God. The Great Commission commands us to 'go and make disciples of all nations, baptising them in the name of the Father and of the Son and of the Holy Spirit, and teaching them to obey everything I have commanded you' (Matthew 28:19–20). How can the teachings of our Saviour be proclaimed if the people of God are denied the Word of God which they need in order to be true disciples of Christ? Mark 16:15–16 exhorts us to 'Go into all the world and preach the good news to all creation'. There are no exceptions. The Word of God must be available to all humankind, in the four corners of the world.

The decision about Bible-smuggling is one that each Christian must make in good faith, before the God he seeks to honour, serve and glorify.

For some facts and figures about Russia today, see p. 134.

2

POLAND, 1987
To Hel and back

Poland today is one of the most Catholic countries in the world. It became a state in AD 966. In the sixteenth century, Protestantism spread to Poland with first the Lutherans and then the Calvinists. Reformation movements took root among townsfolk of German origin, the aristocracy and the rich gentry. A law passed in Sejm in 1573 granted Catholics and Protestants equal freedom of faith.

The greatest threat to Polish Catholicism came at the end of the eighteenth century, when Poland was partitioned among its three neighbours, Austria, Russia and Prussia. For 123 years the Polish state disappeared from the map of Europe. During these years of captivity a unique combination of religious faith and patriotism took root in the popular mind. In the second half of the nineteenth century, various free-church movements began to spread throughout partitioned Poland. Baptist, Pentecostal and Church of Christ movements became especially vigorous after the First World War. In 1918, Poland regained its independence, and kept it until Hitler invaded on 1 September 1939. Two weeks later the Soviet army attacked Poland from the east, in line with the Molotov-Ribbentrop Pact of August 1939; and Poland was partitioned again, this time between two totalitarian powers. At the end of the Second World War, Poland remained within the Soviet sphere of influence until the grass-roots Solidarity movement helped to establish democracy in 1989.

From 1989, the gradual transition to an export-oriented market economy was slowed by world recession and the difficulty of restructuring unprofitable heavy industry. A painful reform programme is bearing fruit, and by mid-1993 Poland was the first post-Communist economy to show real growth through private enterprise. Unemployment then stood at 14%. Poland is now seeking membership of the European Union.

(Source: *Operation World*)

Beyond the wall

It was at a conference in 1986 that I first met Christians from Poland. I recall one pastor giving me his card. He was the minister of the evangelical church in Szczecin, and he asked me to keep in touch, saying that he would love me to visit and preach at his church. I felt somewhat embarrassed that such an invitation should be offered to me, and inadequate, as I was only a full-time pastoral elder, uneducated at theological college, and totally unaware of the needs of the Polish nation, both material and spiritual.

In fact, all I knew about Poland was the name of Lech Walesa, the shipbuilder, who caused a revolution and brought the whole shipyard to a standstill in 1980. This very bloody conflict had lasted for twenty-one days. Shipyard workers staged a sit-in behind the iron gates of the shipyard. The Communist authorities played a waiting game until the workers' nerves finally snapped, whereupon the military stormed the gates with tanks and submachine guns, leaving many dead in their wake. Lech Walesa and a number of others were imprisoned.

There was something remarkable about this Polish pastor, who was of a similar age to me. He described how his church had grown from thirty to a hundred over the past two years, and had attracted young people who were dissatisfied with Communist lies and were turning to God. I sensed that this was not just a polite invitation, but a desperate hope that we might one day meet again, not in my country, but in his.

Over the next year, I corresponded many times with the pastor, and his invitation burned deeply in my heart. The summer before taking up a place at Spurgeon's College in London, I made a ten-day visit to Poland with a church worship leader and friend, Chris Letts.

We travelled via Berlin, where we had time to observe the contrast that existed between East and West. The bright colours and Parisian-style cafés of West Berlin seemed to shout to the whole of Eastern Europe, 'Look what you're missing!' Looking down from the telecommunications tower in the heart of the city, it was amazing to see the strip of mined land separating East Germany from this small outpost of West Germany, protected by many towers, spotlights, dogs and guards.

That night, on a train to Szczecin, the contrast struck us further. A few hours earlier we had been surrounded by bright lights, music and every sign of affluence, which oozed out of each crevice and corner of West Berlin (in an obnoxious sort of way). Now we were surrounded by dull, grey blocks of flats crumbling from lack of care and investment. It was as if there had been a massive power cut. Maybe there had been, because there were hardly any lights on in the flats. It was eerie that there were no people to be seen anywhere, even though it was a Saturday night. The difference that the border made between East and West was indeed dramatic.

We arrived at Szczecin's large, grey, dirty and deserted station in the small hours of Sunday morning. We were somewhat jet-lagged and train-lagged as we landed in this new country and unknown town. We were also somewhat disconcerted that we could not see anybody waiting for us. We waited for fifteen minutes, contemplating the possibilities of a night spent at a railway station, when the pastor and his son finally arrived. They took us to our accommodation, which was on the fifth floor of one of the blocks of flats. There were about a hundred steps to climb in complete darkness, struggling with our heavy bags. We wanted to have a quick wash and get into bed, but we were not allowed to do so until we had been fed and watered. We could not believe the big meal prepared for us – soup, cabbage, potatoes and meat, followed by strawberries with sugar.

We were told that we would have to leave for the morning service in five hours' time.

We breakfasted on the leftovers from the night's meal as well as bread, jam and cheese. East Europeans often have very few resources, but they offer their guests absolutely everything that they have in their home, even if it means going without themselves.

Suitably attired in jackets, trousers and ties, outside the block of flats we found a battered old Mercedes waiting to deliver us to the church. People were making their way through the quiet and wet cobbled street to the old, crumbling church building with a Victorian-style façade. Inside were many neat rows of wooden pews, a pulpit, and a hundred or so people eagerly praying for God's blessing upon the service. They had been there for as much as two hours already. The service itself lasted just over two hours, with much singing, and preaching from the pastor and myself. We shared holy communion, an occasion I found very moving, as it reminded me that God's people are one family irrespective of nationality.

The land of the Black Madonna

As we spent time with our hosts over the next couple of days, Chris and I had the opportunity to hand out Polish tracts, to which we got a mixed response.

One sunny evening, as we walked around the tower block where we were staying, we came across some young people in a park. Chris had his guitar, and we started singing some old Beatles numbers. Within seconds we were surrounded by around fifty young people, all staring at us as if we had come from Mars. One or two spoke English, and we told them where we were from and why we had come to Poland. We sang some Christian songs, taught them some children's songs, and gave them tracts. It was one of the spontaneous highlights of the trip. We prayed that as a result many of them would come to know Christ as their Lord and Saviour in the days that lay ahead.

The next day, members of the church took us on a forty-mile drive to the northern coastline of Poland, which meets the Baltic Sea. We stopped *en route* at a famous monastery, which honoured the Black Madonna of Poland, the sacred icon of Our Lady kept at the shrine of Jasna Gora in Czestochowa, and revered by Catholic Poles as the Queen of Poland. Wherever we went in this country we were to see paintings and photographs of the Black Madonna, who was supposed to have special healing powers.

In 1957 Cardinal Wyszynski had initiated a remarkable nine-year spiritual renewal called the Great Novena, which culminated in 1966 with the thousandth anniversary of Christianity in Poland. The entire Catholic population renewed vows of loyalty to God and the Virgin Mary (originally made by King Kazimierz in 1656 after a few Polish noblemen had successfully defended the monastery of Czestochowa against Swedish forces). Polish bishops dedicated the country to the Virgin Mary for the freedom of the church, both in Poland and throughout the world. The authorities did everything they could to impede the Novena and the millennium celebrations. When the church announced the theme of the celebrations – faithfulness to God, the cross and the gospels – the authorities responded by removing crucifixes from schools. In answer to the church's defence of the life of the soul and the body, they passed more liberal abortion laws. The icon of the Black Madonna was confiscated several times and finally confined indefinitely to Czestochowa.

The home of Solidarity

We headed the next day for Gdansk in the far northeastern corner of Poland, to preach in another church there. Gdansk is home of much of Poland's culture and heritage and was also the scene of the shipyard revolution of 1982. In 1980 the Solidarity Free Trade Union was formed in an ever-worsening economic climate, under the leadership of Lech Walesa. Many observers of the shipyard sit-in were confused by banners carrying pictures of the Madonna and the Pope, which were hung on the shipyard gates, and by the sight of workers kneeling in the open to receive holy communion. The Polish workers' revolution cannot be explained exclusively in economic or even political terms, for Solidarity, some maintain, was in essence a spiritual revolution, a reaction in a Christian spirit to the violation of human dignity and human rights. The spiritual value of truth was at the centre of the protest as Solidarity fought against the falsehood of the Communist system.

When we arrived at Gdansk railway station, we were met by the pastor and a friend of his who took us to their Evangelical church's premises. These were quite vast, seating approximately five hundred people, and housing offices and sleeping quarters for guests. After a delicious meal in the kitchen, lovingly prepared by the staff, we went for a walk around the area. We saw yet more blocks of flats and a great deal of repair work being done on the roads. This area on the edge of Gdansk suffered much from dilapidation.

The following day we met the church's leaders, and were given a guided tour of the church premises along with an update on the Christian scene in this former capital. Our young guide spoke very good English, and included in her tour the shipyard, where we saw the memorial to those who had died in the revolution, a monument made of steel in the shape of three crosses. Hundreds of candles burnt daily as a constant reminder of the great sacrifice these people had made, and to keep their desire for peace alive in the hearts and minds of those living.

We spent some time looking round a number of museums and admiring the architecture of this beautiful city, before returning to the church for an evening service which had been arranged specially for our visit. We preached on two consecutive nights to congregations of around two hundred.

'You go to Hel'

On our second day in Gdansk, the pastor's wife, with whom we were staying, suggested we take a hydrofoil trip across the harbour before the next service, while she went to meet someone. We bought our tickets and enjoyed the ride for half an hour before realizing that we were going too far out to sea. We rushed to find out where we were going, but could find no-one who could speak English, until we were directed to a young man in the boiler room, called Andre. He was very excited, as he had been learning English for over two years but had never met an English person before.

I asked him a clear, simple question, 'Where are we going?'

His response was not what we expected. 'You go to Hel.'

I thought he had misunderstood me so I repeated myself, but he gave the same answer. 'The place we go is Hel.'

It transpired that we were in fact going to Hel, and that it would take longer to get there and back than we had left before our church service began.

Andre became our shadow. We explained our difficulty, and he said confidently, 'No problem.' He took us to the captain, who eagerly pulled back the throttle and got us back to Gdansk with ten minutes to spare.

As we sped along, we chatted with Andre amid the roar of the engines and the white spray of sea, and shared with him what it meant to be a Christian. We prayed with him and he received Christ. 'Make sure you preach really well and many come to know Jesus tonight,' he said to us as we leapt off the hydrofoil at Gdansk harbour. We rushed to the church, where we found every head bowed and the preacher praying for our return. Word had got around that we would be there, and many more people had come to hear us preach and sing. There were smiles and hallelujahs when they opened their eyes and saw that we had made it.

We later learned that Andre had started going to church, had been baptized and had become a strong Christian. Over the next five years I would receive postcards from ports all over Europe from Andre saying how he was getting on and thanking us for telling him about Jesus.

Catholic and Protestant

The next stop on our tour was Warsaw, where we first visited the Baptist Seminary, at that time poorly lacking in essential resources. We visited a number of Catholic churches, including St Stanislave Kostka where the thirty-seven-year-old priest and martyr, Father Jerzy Popieluszko, had served. Fr Popieluszko was framed by secret police who, in December 1983, accused him of harbouring an immense illegal arsenal. He was released, but an intense campaign against him was mounted by the media. He was found dead, floating in the Vistula river in October 1984. His grave and the church crypt remain a place of pilgrimage.

We also visited a number of Orthodox churches found in the old part of Warsaw. The Polish Autocephalous Orthodox Church is still the largest non-Catholic religious group in Poland, with more than three hundred churches and chapels and six monastic houses. The Orthodox Church of Poland was formed as a branch of the Moscow Patriarchate in 1918.

Another major church in Poland is the Ukraine-based Eastern Rite Catholic Church, which owes its origins to the Uniate

Church (Orthodox in liturgy but in communion with Rome). This church was formed in the 1590s by Ukrainian and Belarussian members of the Orthodox hierarchy who had transferred their allegiance from Constantinople, the seat of Orthodoxy, to Rome, the seat of Catholicism.

In June 1984, Archbishop Myroslav S. Marusyn, Secretary of the Vatican Congregation for the Eastern Churches, visited Poland by invitation of the Primate as a representative of the Pope, the first such visit since the Second World War. Many Ukrainians interpreted this visit as a major step towards legal recognition of the Eastern Rite in Poland.

In the early 1970s, the Light-Life movement, a synthesis of general renewal movements in the church, developed rapidly, largely under the direction of Fr Franciszek Blachnicki. Oasis retreat camps and renewal youth movements within the Catholic Church attracted hundreds of thousands of nominal Catholics, who came to have a warm faith in Christ as a result of Bible study groups, camps and the printing of Christian literature.

While we were in Warsaw we saw the results of this for ourselves when we preached in another church, which was full of young people. There were some two hundred people inside, and another hundred or so peering in from outside or standing at the back for the whole two hours.

Since our trip in 1987, it has been fascinating to watch the immense changes that have taken place in the circumstances of this resilient nation. In the first free elections in the Soviet bloc in 1989, the Communists were heavily defeated in Poland. Two years later, Lech Walesa was elected president.

In January 1991, the Catholic Church held a conference for over twenty-five thousand priests to prepare them to evangelize the young people of Poland. The summer before, the Oasis renewal group attracted seventy-three thousand young people to their summer activities. The church has also become more involved in politics, social issues and helping to rebuild the economy.

The first March for Jesus took place in Poland in 1992.

The Catholic Church was the custodian of Polish culture and nationalism in the face of Russian imperialism and Soviet Communism. It successfully blocked all efforts by the Communists to deprive it of its independence and to foist atheism on the

nation. It is theologically conservative and has regained a powerful political influence since the fall of Communism. The election
of a Pole, John Paul II, to the papacy is indicative of the influence
religious leaders may have.

On 19 November 1995 President Lech Walesa was narrowly
defeated by forty-one-year-old Aleksander Kwasniewski. This
placed former Communists in effective control of presidency,
government and Parliament, and was widely expected to signal a
period of church–state confrontation. The result was also seen as a
serious pastoral failure by Poland's predominant Roman Catholic
Church, whose leader, Cardinal Jozef Glemp of Warsaw, had
publicly described the contest as one between 'Christian and neo-
pagan values'. This national dominant Catholic stance has caused
many difficulties for evangelical churches throughout Poland,
often resulting in their being denied land on which to build
churches, or the possibility of hiring public buildings for
evangelical worship services. January 1996 church figures suggest
that regular Mass attendance has declined to around 33% of
Catholics, compared to 37.8% in 1990. Other statistics suggest
that vocations to the priesthood have fallen by a third from their
1985–7 high point. Evangelical churches are encouraged by
growth in the number of churches and in church membership,
and an increase in social-care projects, evangelism and Bible
colleges like the Baptist Theological Seminary in Warsaw-Radosc.
Evangelicals and charismatic Christians, however, are a small
percentage of the population compared to the Roman Catholic
Church.

Some facts and figures: Poland today

	Congregations	Members	Affiliated
Roman Catholic	8,573	23,700,000	35,377,000
Orthodox	451	496,000	800,000
Augsburg Confession	352	68,300	91,000
Seventh Day Adventist	130	10,000	40,000
Assemblies of God	143	12,400	16,500
Methodist	50	3,500	7,000
Polish Baptist Union	56	3,150	5,000
Reformed Evangelical	17	2,800	4,000

	Congregations	Members	Affiliated
Jehovah's Witnesses	248	96,841	161,000
Other churches	360	16,780	4,523

Number of estimated missionaries to Poland: 77 associated with 25 mission agencies, *i.e.* 1 for every 500,000 people.

Number of estimated missionaries from Poland: 67 associated with 5 mission agencies, *i.e.* 1 in every 2,800 Polish Protestants.

The Methodist Church was established in Poland by Americans in 1920. The United Evangelical Church was established in 1947 out of autonomous churches including Pentecostals. The Lutheran Church is also strong in Poland, with 73,818 members and 331 churches. There are more Jehovah's Witnesses in Poland than there are evangelicals. New Age and eastern religious movements, occultism and materialism are gaining ground and growing rapidly, especially among the young and disillusioned. Bible training for leaders is developing fast. By 1993 there were twenty Protestant institutions, remarkable for a land where Protestants form such a small minority.

(Source: *Operation World*)

3

HUNGARY, 1975, 1988 AND TODAY
The struggle for freedom

Hungary was once much larger than it is today. In 896, seven Magyar tribes under Chief Arpad swept in from beyond the Volga river and occupied the Danube basin. They terrorized Europe with raids as far as France and Italy, until their conversion to Roman Catholicism in the late tenth century.

Hungary's first king and patron saint, Stephen I, was crowned on Christmas Day in the year 1000, marking the foundation of the Hungarian state. After the Mongols sacked Hungary in 1241, many cities were fortified. Feudal Hungary was a large and powerful state, which included Transylvania (in present Romania) and Croatia (formerly part of Yugoslavia). The great imperial city has known its hardships. It has suffered at the hands of the Turks, who, after bitter conflict, left the city with a few bathhouses in Buda and a couple of mosques in Pecs (pronounced Pesh).

Hungary lost 60% of its land at the break-up of the Austro-Hungarian Empire in 1918, leaving large Hungarian minorities living in surrounding countries. During the Second World War Hungary was occupied by the Russian army, which left only in 1991. A Russian-engineered coup brought the Communists to power in 1947. Hungary was the first Communist-controlled Eastern European country to abandon Marxism and institute a multi-party democracy, which it did in 1991.

The first freely elected government brought economic and political stability, but disillusionment has eroded the high expectations which many Hungarians held for the future. Hungary was the first Communist-bloc state to begin privatizing the economy, and the first ex-Communist-bloc state to record positive economic growth. It is poor in natural resources, but has a developed industrial base and productive agricultural land. The human cost of change and recovery from the mismanagement and large public debt generated by the Communist regime is high. By December 1992, unemployment rose to 11% and public debt to US $2,050 per head.

1975: ordered to leave

Without question Hungary is the most accessible Eastern European country. Only a short hop from Vienna, this romantic land of Franz Liszt, Bela Bartok, Gypsy music and the Blue Danube welcomes visitors. I believe Budapest to be one of the most enchanting cities of Europe. The fine wines, fiery paprika, sweet violins, good theatre and colourful folklore, and the friendliness of the Magyars, are as inviting as their renowned goulash soup.

My first visit to Hungary was in the summer of 1975 as a twenty-year-old on a tour of Europe. I was immediately impressed by the beautiful splendour of its magnificent capital. The city spans both sides of the Danube, and a string of six ornate bridges links both halves: Pest, the poorer, industrial half, and Buda, the more affluent area, which occupies the high ground (the castle district) to the west of the city. Magnificent parliamentary buildings adorn the eastern banks of the Danube, along with a number of splendid Catholic and Orthodox churches (St Stephen's is of especial note). It was interesting to see that even in 1975, a number of western companies were beginning to invest in Hungary. The narrow streets and little gift shops were intriguing, as were the many bright yellow trams that rattled around the city at tremendous speed. These trams were one of Hungary's major exports to its neighbours in the eastern bloc.

On my first evening in Budapest I found myself in a park on the Buda side of the city, close to its ancient castle. Preparations were under way for a pop concert. I joined the five hundred other young people who were surrounded by guards with sub-machine guns as the pop group belted out its renditions of western-style pop music. The young people were not allowed to move or dance, but they could clap at the end of each song.

After the concert, some of us went into the city together, and I was invited back to the house of a young lad called Tony for a meal and to stay the night.

The next morning I awoke to a tremendous commotion. Tony and his parents were having a heated debate in the kitchen. I discovered later that his parents were annoyed with Tony for letting a westerner stay in their home. This was against the law in Communist Hungary. They were genuinely frightened, while wanting to be hospitable. Tony asked me how long I was allowed to stay in Hungary, which I thought a strange question. When we established that I did not have a permit to be there, Tony went rather pale and said, 'You have registered as a westerner at the police station, haven't you?'

'No,' I said. I had not known I had to.

'You must register immediately you arrive in the country,' he said, 'so that they know you are here; and you have to get your permit stamped when you leave the country.' We went straight to the police station, where, unfortunately, the desk sergeant was playing everything by the book. I was placed in a secure room and my backpack was confiscated. About an hour later somebody arrived from the British Embassy and stamped one or two forms. I was immediately placed in a car, taken to the railway station and ordered to leave the country.

1988: curtains on bits of string

It was not until the summer of 1988 that I made a return visit to Hungary *en route* to Romania. This trip was the result of a telephone call from a contact at the Baptist Union about the visit of a Hungarian youth choir to Britain. Because of my interest in Eastern Europe, I was invited to meet the choir while they were here. I jumped at the opportunity, and as I listened to their beautiful singing, I found myself sitting next to a pastor from Romania. He gave me his name and address and invited me to preach in his church, after hinting briefly at the desperate material and spiritual needs of his country. He indicated that any help I could give would be of tremendous encouragement.

At the same event, I met a Hungarian pastor and his eighteen-year-old daughter, Rebecca, who made the same invitation, as did the Rev. Emil Kiss, President of the Baptist Union in Hungary.

By the end of the week, with my family and our friends, Roger and Doreen Brown, I had packed up the car and was driving to Hungary.

Once in Budapest, I rang Rebecca, who directed us to her church, where she met us. She took us to meet her family and found us a place to stay in a Baptist guest house. A guided tour of the Baptist seminary later the next day revealed a contrast with the facilities available at Spurgeon's College, where I was a student. Bedrooms were small and accommodated six students each. Their desks were divided by curtains hanging on bits of string. The library had very few theological books. But there was hope, as the Baptists had been granted permission to build a new seminary in the grounds of the old college. We were able to see for ourselves the foundations of the building then being constructed by members of the Baptist Church and friends of the seminary. Money from the Baptist World Alliance and the European Baptist Federation helped to buy the materials needed.

That evening we spoke and sang at a mid-week prayer meeting. The next day we met with Emil Kiss and the Baptist Union of Hungary's General Secretary, the Rev. Janos Viczian, who gave us an update on the growth of Baptists in Hungary and their present needs. As we arrived at the old grey building in downtown Budapest, we had to climb over a number of people sitting and crowding round the entrance to the Baptist Union, who we guessed must be local Gypsies. We later discovered that they were refugees from Romania who had managed to escape the harsh regime of Ceaucescu by either swimming across the river that runs along the border of Romania and Hungary, or hiding underneath or on the roofs of trains. They were the lucky ones. The unlucky had been shot and killed trying to escape. We were told that there was a great need for food and clothes for these refugees. The Hungarians were trying to help them as much as possible out of their own meagre resources.

From Budapest we drove through flat countryside towards the Romanian border. Hungary had lost a great deal of land to

Romania after the First World War. This particular part of Europe used to be known as its bread basket, because of the great prairie-like fields where mile upon mile of wheat was grown to produce bread not only for the Hungarians, but for other nations too. Now Hungary had to import wheat from the rest of Europe, and Hungarians felt robbed of the land that now fell in Romania, a situation which has caused much unrest and antagonism between the two countries.

Some Hungarian history

The end of the First World War gave Hungary independence from Austria, but deprived it of two-thirds of its territory, not only to Romania but also to Czechoslovakia and Yugoslavia. In 1941, the Hungarians' desire to recover their lost territories drew the country into the war alongside the Nazis. When Admiral Miklos Horthy tried to make a separate peace pact with the Allies in October 1944, the occupying army put the German Fascist Arrow Cross party in power. By April 1945, the Hungarians had been liberated by the Soviet army, and in 1948 the Communist and Social Democratic Parties merged to become the Hungarian Workers' Party.

During the early 1950s, Hungary followed the Stalinist line of collectivized agriculture and heavy industry. On 23 October 1956, Soviet troops participated in the suppression of student demonstrations in Budapest which had caused a general rebellion. A full-scale Soviet invasion was conducted on 4 November, but fighting continued, and two hundred thousand Hungarians fled to Austria.

After the revolt, the Hungarian Socialist Workers' Party was reorganized and Janos Kadar took over as President. Hungary has always been one of the most independent members of the Soviet bloc and was one of the first to institute reforms. The Hungarian government's decision in 1989, to allow East German refugees to cross the Hungarian borders into the West, played a crucial role in the overthrow of the East German government and the break-down of Communist Eastern Europe as a whole.

The forty years of bondage may now be over, but the moral, social and spiritual damage of Marxism still blights the country, and, sadly, the church. Although some Catholic and Protestant leaders boldly stood for the Lord and suffered, some official church leaders retained their position only by compromising with Communist authorities. A legacy of suspicion, mistrust and division is the result.

Among those who stood up for their faith was the Catholic Primate, Cardinal Jozsef Mindeszenty, who, in 1948, spoke out against the Communist regime, and was arrested, subjected to a notorious trial and sent to prison, along with six hundred other priests. All of the nation's church schools (3,150 in number, about half the national whole) were taken over by the Communists. In 1950, more than ten thousand monks and nuns were thrown out of their monasteries and convents overnight and subjected to years of humiliation, imprisonment and torture. There is no accurate record of the number who died while in prison.

During the 1956 uprising, Cardinal Mindeszenty, who by then had spent eight years in prison, took refuge in the American Embassy, where he lived for the next fifteen years. His residence there proved a great embarrassment to the Vatican, since it prevented the Hungarian Catholic Church from gaining any concessions. Eventually, in 1974, Pope Paul VI removed him from office, and he died, a broken-hearted man, the following year.

The first agreement between the Communist government and the Vatican was signed in 1964. It was very limited. During the 1960s, arrests and secret trials continued for the 'offences' of evangelizing and spreading religious views or instructing the young. As late as 1971, four priests and a female student were given sentences of up to five years for evangelizing. One of these priests committed suicide. Priests' licences were frequently revoked. For instance, in 1965, a thousand priests (almost 20% of the total number) were excluded from pastoral activities.

The state controlled the churches and the spread of religion to a tremendous degree, as reflected by a fall in the number of Catholic children registered for religious education from 90% in 1957 to a mere 6% in 1975. Although its legal powers were perhaps less far-reaching than those of parallel institutions in Czechoslovakia, Romania and Poland, they were quite stringent.

The churches and the authorities

Hungary had revivals in 1939 and 1946 through to 1950, which touched the Reformed and other Free Churches. There are now several strong charismatic and renewal movements in the Catholic Church and the Baptist, Reformed and Free Churches, and also a Pietist Bible Union within the Reformed Church, to which 130 of the church's 850 pastors belong. There are growing independent charismatic congregations, and also a flourishing intercessory movement.

Christians in Hungary had less to fear than in most other eastern-bloc countries. They were not in physical danger, though they could lose their jobs or chances of promotion. This resulted in a high proportion of elderly churchgoers who had no job to lose, though more and more people did risk attending church, despite the fact that no-one could be a member of the Party and a Christian. The press made frequent references at the time to Party officials who had been reprimanded for showing up in church on family occasions.

In the 1960s and 70s, the state began to accept that some evangelism might actually be useful in promoting positive ethical values. The first religious bookshop was opened in Budapest in 1977. As young people became disillusioned with Marxism and Leninism, widespread despair threatened the stability of the country, and even Christianity was seen by the government as having a potentially useful role. In the 1980s, churches were able to invite western speakers such as Billy Graham and Nicky Cruz to lead missions, and there was no need for a believer to be without a Bible. Religious education, once banned in schools, was reinstated and promoted. Hungarian churches were very active in social care, particularly with the handicapped and the elderly, a practice which prepared them to care for the large number of refugees who fled to Hungary from Romania in 1988.

Despite such allowances, the attitude of the authorities towards religion remained ambivalent. In 1987, a Hungarian psychologist expressed concern about the number of young people who refused any positive values and who, apparently out of despera-tion, worshipped Satan. The only solution, said the psychologist, is to show them the real value of what the church can do. However, she went on to say that the authorities, afraid that the churches might have real influence, seemed to prefer young people to remain unhappy rather than to be converted. In the meantime, Satanism, violence and hatred were becoming more widespread among the young, she believed; and as a result the suicide rate was increasing.

The situation was not helped by discontent within the churches. Tension in the Lutheran Church came to a head at the Lutheran World Federation meeting in 1984, which took place in Budapest. Although Lutherans represented only 4% of the Hungarian population, the controversial theology of *diakonia* (service), which Bishop Kaldy proposed, had far-reaching significance, and was taken on board by other major churches as well. It taught that the church had a responsibility to support the government without dissent, putting itself at the government's service.

'There is no third way for travellers, between socialism and capitalism,' Kaldy said. 'Our Protestant churches are not neutral; we stand unambiguously on the side of socialism.'

A similar line was taken by Cardinal Leakai, whose 'small steps' policy revolved around his cautious belief that full co-operation with the government would gradually lead to small improvements in the life of the church.

Until 1986, church leaders were silent, no doubt under state instructions about the oppression of their fellow Hungarians, but some church members were deeply concerned and helped quietly.

Hungary in the 1990s

By May 1988, there were approximately sixty thousand refugees from Ceaucescu's wrecked Romania in Hungary, many in desperate need of food, shelter and employment. All three major churches – Catholic, Reformed and Lutheran – were opening busy refugee centres. The campaign for aid saw Hungarians and Romanians co-operating in a remarkable way.

In 1991, property confiscated from churches was returned, and those priests still imprisoned were released and rehabilitated at government expense.

Before the Holocaust, there were 725,000 Jews in Hungary, many of them refugees from Hitler's Germany. Now their number is down to eighty thousand. Anti-Semitism is still a problem which needs to be purged from the nation, although Hungarian Jews are the largest and most favoured Jewish community in Eastern Europe. They have the only rabbinical seminary in the former Communist bloc, which trains rabbis from other countries, including the former Soviet Union. Many of the hundred synagogues are well attended. There are twenty-six rabbis, a number of secondary schools, a hospital and two old peoples' homes. Young Jews are increasingly marrying non-Jews, however, and show little enthusiasm for their heritage and faith.

There are some hopeful signs among the Gypsy community as new charismatic fellowships are established there.

One of the biggest problems of the mid-90s was the flood of refugees from war-torn Yugoslavia, which added an extra burden to the nation. Economic difficulties have created stress, pessimism and concern for the future. Many have fallen prey to alcoholism, suicide, burgeoning cults and the occult because of their ignorance of sin and the gospel. Many of the denominations are experiencing a leadership crisis, and fresh inspiration is needed all round.

Nevertheless, a new day is now dawning in this country. For Christians living in secular societies, ecumenism should be an imperative, but in Hungary it existed only by chance. But now, where links were virtually non-existent, some denominations are working together in social-action projects, helping the poor, refugees, drug addicts and the homeless. The Reformed Church began a telephone counselling service in Budapest in 1984, and has opened a home for alcoholics and delinquent youths, which complements the successful work of the Free Churches (Baptist and Pentecostal) in evangelizing Gypsies. The impressive changes made in the way of life of many Gypsies has attracted considerable media coverage. The Baptist and Pentecostal churches are growing considerably, as are many more charismatic churches with a strong focus on evangelism.

Some facts and figures: Hungary today

In 1995, the population of Hungary was 10,509,000, of whom 92% were Magyars (Hungarians). The population of the capital, Budapest, was 2,113,600.

Hungarians living in other lands

Romania	2,252,000
Slovakia	620,000
Serbia	460,000
Ukraine	160,000
Other (including USA)	1,400,000

Minority groups in Hungary

Gypsies	320,000
Ukrainians	300,000
Germans	250,000
Slovaks	100,000
Jews	80,000
Croats	25,000
Poles	21,000
Serbs	20,000
Others (including Chinese)	30,000

	Congregations	Members	Affiliated
Reformed	1,133	500,000	2,000,000
Lutheran	341	113,000	450,000
Baptist	400	10,994	25,000
Nazarenes	100	12,000	20,000
Faith Fellowship	8	5,000	13,000
Assemblies of God	215	4,755	12,000
Seventh Day Adventists	111	5,599	11,200
Apostolic	130	3,000	10,000
Methodist	73	3,000	5,000
Christian Brethren	27	2,000	3,000
Roman Catholic	2,226	4,880,000	6,508,000
Romanian Orthodox	18	10,900	16,500
Jehovah's Witnesses	238	10,647	15,200

Missionaries in Hungary: 21, associated with 33 agencies, *i.e.* 1 to every 50,000 Hungarians.
(Source: *Operation World*)

4

ROMANIA, 1987-9
The shadow of Ceaucescu

Romania is a Balkan state on the lower River Danube, surrounded by
Bulgaria in the south, Moldavia in the east, Hungary in the west and
Slovakia in the north. It was formed in 1862 when Moldavia and
Wallachia joined together under the kingship of Alexandru Ioan
Cuza. The reform-minded Cuza was forced to abdicate four years
later. His place was taken by the Prussian prince, Carol I. With
Russian assistance, Romania declared independence from the
Ottoman Empire in 1877, after the War of Independence which
ceded Dobrogea to the young Romania. In 1916, Romania entered
the First World War on the side of the Allies with the objective of
taking Transylvania, where two-thirds of the population were
Romanian, from Austro-Hungary. During the fighting, the central
powers occupied Wallachia, but Moldavia was defended staunchly
by Romanian and Russian troops. With the defeat of Austro-Hungary
in 1918, the unification of Transylvania, Bukovina and Banat with
Romania was finally achieved.

In the years leading up to the Second World War, Romania sought
security in an alliance with France and Britain. It also signed a pact
with Yugoslavia, Turkey and Greece, and established diplomatic
relations with the USSR. These efforts were weakened when King
Carol II declared a personal dictatorship in 1938. By the time France
fell in May 1940, Romania was isolated.

The Soviet Union occupied Bessarabia and northern Bukovina (the
area taken from Russia after the First World War) in June 1940.

Then, on 30 August 1940, Romania was forced to cede northern Transylvania (with its 43,500 square kilometres and 2.6 million inhabitants) to Hungary by order of Nazi Germany and Fascist Italy. This sparked a widespread demonstration, forcing King Carol II to abdicate in favour of his son Michael, and a Fascist dictatorship was imposed. German troops were allowed to enter Romania in October 1940. On 23 August 1944, Romania suddenly changed sides (capturing fifty-three thousand German soldiers present in Romania at the time) and declared war on Nazi Germany. With this dramatic act, Romania salvaged its independence and shortened the war. By 25 October, the Romanian and Soviet armies had driven the Hungarians and the Germans from Transylvania. The Romanian army went on to fight in Hungary and Czechoslovakia.

Half a million Romanian soldiers died in the war. After national liberation was won, the government of Dr Petru Groza launched Romania's social liberation, with progressive parties winning the parliamentary elections of November 1946. A year later, the monarchy was abolished and a Romanian people's republic proclaimed.

Romania is a land rich in agriculture, minerals and oil, but much of its valuable natural resources were plundered, impoverished and polluted under Communist rule for the benefit of the elite. Economic liberalization since 1990 has been slow because of reluctance on the part of the government, and a bureaucratic system which strangles progress.

The Communists took control of Romania in 1947 after a coup supported by the Soviet Union. They succeeded in creating one of the Communist bloc's most oppressive and cruel regimes, and even the revolution of 1989–90 failed to unseat the Communist leadership. A rejuvenated secret police still exists and exercises a persuasive control. An anti-minorities nationalism against Hungarians and Gypsies is on the rise.

Under Communist rule, the churches were manipulated and controlled, and those which refused to submit were severely oppressed. Religious freedom is now guaranteed, but legislation passed in 1991 recognizes only fourteen religious bodies as eligible for state subsidies, and instituted a system that could be used to exert government control in a way which could hinder the work of certain denominations and evangelistic groups.

The revolution of 1989–90 removed the Ceaucescu 'dynasty' but did not eradicate the Marxist approach to government, while the years of Communist rule created a great spiritual thirst. Growth among Baptists, Pentecostals and Brethren has been marked for the past two decades, and began to accelerate markedly in 1989, with an estimated sixteen hundred churches planted in just three years. A spirit of revival pervades many areas of church life. Luís Palau and other western evangelists have been used by God to win many for Christ through crusades in this country.

The Orthodox Church is opposed to Protestant growth, having lost some members. One Orthodox leader is said to have called Protestantism the biggest heresy in Europe. But a remarkable and unofficial renewal movement within the Orthodox Church, the Lord's Army, has arisen in recent years. It has around three hundred thousand members and many more sympathizers, and is particularly strong in northern rural areas.

There is a great need for Bible teaching, as few pastors have had any formal training. As many as 80% of Pentecostal pastors, for example, are not formally trained. As a result, petty legalism is common, sermon preparation is often despised, and a strong emphasis is placed on the prophetic word over the Scriptures. There are also ethnic divisions, as Romanians and the large Hungarian minority do not get on well together. Members of the Gypsy community are also ill-treated.

Materialism, imported from the West, has damaged the nation spiritually, and alcoholism, unemployment, drug abuse, prostitution, pornography, violence, theft, glue-sniffing and homelessness are increasingly common.

On the plus side, improvements have been made to the Baptist seminary in Bucharest, so that where once it was possible to train only six students, a hundred can now be accommodated. Another Baptist seminary has opened in Oradea. Many more Christians are being trained in children's ministry, counselling and theology.

After the collapse of Communism, a profusion of agencies, congregations and individuals rushed into Romania to help. While much that was achieved was good and worthwhile, many went in with little tact and less wisdom, to teach, dispense favours and manipulate. It is important to pray that expatriates working in Romania and other Eastern European countries show sensitivity, humility and an ability to learn from their work alongside Romanian Christians. Long-term incarnational ministry for the growth of the church is more important than making short forays in to alleviate an ongoing need.

On 28 February 1997, King Michael of Romania officially returned to his country to a hero's welcome, fifty years after his expulsion. King Michael, now seventy-five, ruled Romania between 1926 and 1930 and was known as 'the boy king'. A crowd of ten thousand gathered in University Square, Bucharest, chanting 'Long live King Michael' and 'The monarchy will save Romania'. Although the turnout was significantly lower than the hundred thousand who greeted him when he returned briefly while still a non-Romanian citizen in 1992, the warmth of the welcome was none the less genuine. At the airport the king and his wife were accorded a traditional welcome, including a gift of bread and salt, a symbol of hospitality. They were met by Prime Minister Viktor Ciorbea and several other government ministers. The king received his Romanian passport issued in the name of Michael of Romania. Officially, King Michael's return to Romania was as a private person. A statement he put out before the visit said, 'I shall not raise any constitutional or material matter. I come to you not to take but to give, not to divide but to unite.' But, for most of the supporters who gathered in Bucharest, the restoration of a constitutional monarchy would seem the best guarantee of freedom and democracy in a country that has been subjected to some of the worst excesses of Communism and Fascism.

1987: poverty and desolation

In chapter 3 I described how four of us drove across Hungary *en route* for Romania. Just before reaching the Romanian border on our way out of Hungary, we stopped the car at a wooded area, as we had been advised by other Christians who had visited the country, to hide our Bibles and Christian music tapes, not only for our own protection but also for that of the Romanian Christians with whom we would have contact. We put them in a carrier bag and buried them in the wood. At the border, we watched, as Ruth and I had done on the drive into Russia, as a car in front of us was pulled apart. When it was our turn to pass the checkpoint, we were asked to take our six suitcases off the roof and open them. They were full of food, which, we explained, were gifts for some Romanian friends. After about half an hour, we were waved through.

It took us about two hours to drive the first twenty miles, as we were so amazed by what we saw. Everywhere we looked, there was complete desolation and poverty, such as we had not seen anywhere else in Europe. Children were lining the streets in the villages, waving and shouting to us in what we mistakenly thought was a welcome. We later discovered that they were begging for food. We saw women washing their clothes in rivers, and men and women working hard in the fields, driving oxen and carts laden with hay. In one village, we bought some tomatoes, and were invited into the home of the vegetable grower, where we saw great activity going on in the courtyard. A pig had been killed and sausages were being made for the winter months, some of which were offered to us. We found the Romanian villagers very friendly, but also suspicious of us, as if they could not imagine why we would want to drive fifteen hundred miles across Europe to come to their country.

When we got to Cluj-Napoca, we called the pastor I had met in England, to be greeted with caution and extreme disbelief that we were actually there. The pastor's son, John, met us at the Hotel Napoca, where we had discovered that the rooms cost US $100 a night, more than we could afford. John told us to wait for him by a lamp-post in the car park. After a nervous and brief greeting he encouraged us to get quickly into the car and drive to his parents' home on an estate of dilapidated high-rise flats. He was an intelligent young man of eighteen who spoke very good English. It was his great desire to leave his country for England, Germany or America, an ambition common among young people in Romania.

I recall being told by a representative of Keston Institute, the research charity which concentrates on religion in Eastern Europe, that it was illegal for Romanians to have westerners in their homes without first seeking official permission from the authorities. John told us not to speak as we moved from the car along the streets to the block of flats where he lived. We went up to the third floor and entered the flat, where we were greeted by John's older sister, Helen, and younger brother, Timothy. Their mother was ill in hospital, and their father away at a conference for the weekend. The curtains were drawn quickly and we were shown into a room where we could all sleep. We could feel the tension in the air as we realized what a risk these young people were taking in offering us hospitality in their home.

The following day, after a good night's rest, John and Helen showed us around Cluj. We looked at the special dollar shop which sold products priced out of the range of the normal Romanian budget, such as hi-fis, radios, fur coats, leather boots, Camel cigarettes, spirits, Walkmans and televisions. We also looked around St Michael's Church, a fifteenth-century Gothic structure with a neo-Gothic tower (1859), which sits in the centre of the Piata Libertatii (Liberty Square).

Along narrow streets, shops were hidden in normal houses. On entering an often very small room, a dark shop could be found, light bulbs being in short supply. Electric lighting was restricted in Romania, and often the nation was plunged into darkness for long periods. Ceaucescu wanted to reduce the country's deficit.

Worship Romanian style

On Sunday we were taken to the Manastur Baptist Church. When we arrived at ten o'clock, the service had been going on for an hour already. Services usually lasted for three hours, with an hour for prayer, an hour for singing and an hour for preaching. Around the outside of the church in the large courtyard were rows and rows of people sitting on benches, listening to the service on a PA system from inside. This was an amazing sight. The church was obviously full, and the only other way to hear God's Word was to sit or stand in the car park on this summer morning, which had reached temperatures of 85–90°C. We reckoned there must be about two hundred people outside the church, and when we squeezed inside we found a further five hundred. Every space was taken: window ledges, pews, chairs down the aisle. The steps up to the pulpit were occupied by children. The balcony was overflowing; there was no more room for anybody.

We were guided by our host (who had warned the leaders that we were coming) to seats in front of the communion table. The six of us – myself, Ruth, our baby daughter Emily, our travelling companions Doreen and Roger, and John – squeezed into a pew made for three to enjoy the service. The church felt like a sauna, as it had no air-conditioning.

A piece of paper was passed from the assistant pastor along the row to me, which read, 'Unfortunately you will not be able to preach, as it is illegal for a westerner to preach in a Romanian church, and we recognize a number of Ceaucescu's secret police (Securitate) in our congregation this morning.' On the reverse side of the paper was written, 'However, we would like you to bring a twenty-minute greeting before we take holy communion together.' It was a great joy to be able to share through John, who interpreted the message. Roger and Doreen sang several songs, which were well appreciated. I was astounded that holy communion was going to be served to over seven hundred people. Two piles of wooden communion trays, each holding a hundred or so glasses, were stacked a yard high on the table, and in each glass a tiny quantity of real wine was measured with an eyedropper. The bread was cut into very tiny cubes. It reminded me that in the West, our problem is not that we have insufficient wine or bread but that we have insufficient communicants.

After the service, we spent a further hour outside the church, sharing the peace, as everybody greeted one another with the word 'Pachy'. There was great rejoicing that we had come to share in their service. One of the deacons, John Achim and his wife Monica, took us home for lunch in their small, sixth-storey flat. We all squeezed into a tiny lift, but unfortunately it had broken down, an apparently regular occurrence.

Once in John and Monica's home, we were surprised to see a baby grand piano. John, Monica and their daughter Joanne were musically gifted, and Monica was a teacher of music and English.

As we relaxed, the couple suddenly burst into rapid Romanian, as John looked out of the window to see that Securitate guards had followed us to the flat and were outside the block in their car, complete with sub-machine gun and binoculars, making copious notes. Our relaxation had been short-lived.

Later, John told us of the Bible training course he ran from his flat. He slid the hatch of a small space above the ceiling tiles, and there, wrapped in a towel, was a Strong's Analytical Concordance, along with several theological books. They remained hidden because the Securitate often raided their flat. John used the books to teach young men in the church who had a desire to preach and to learn about Christian ministry. Sharing with this family, who were obviously being used in a dynamic way for the kingdom of God, was a precious moment.

That afternoon there were many telephone calls from neighbouring churches. John had to be very cautious about what he said, as he knew that his calls were being monitored by the Securitate. As a known Christian activist, he had often been arrested and spent many hours being interrogated by the police.

Before we could leave Romania later that night, we had to preach and minister in a further three churches, each starting an hour after the other. The police were still waiting outside John's flat, but he figured out a way to lose what he called 'these monkeys'. We descended from the flat to our car below, and Monica came with us to give us directions while John drove his car as a decoy. We drove frantically through the streets with Monica shouting, 'Right! Left! Straight ahead! Round this corner!' We were followed until suddenly John went one way and we went another. The police were unsure whom to follow, so they pursued our western vehicle. But within ten minutes we lost them as we took a dirt track alongside a railway line.

We made it to the first church, stayed half an hour, and left for the next, a lively young people's church. From there we went to the third church, where we sensed, on arrival, a great ministry taking place. It was absolutely bursting with about five hundred people (mainly young), and was led by a dynamic twenty-eight-year-old pastor called Benny, who had a ministry to the students at Cluj's university. Many students had been reached through this church. Cluj is known as the 'university city' because there is a big Orthodox theological seminary there, as well as the university itself.

'Supergrannies' across the border

We were asked to stay longer in Cluj to take some services in the week, but we had to return home. At ten o'clock that night we left the church and made our way to the Hungarian border.

We drove along the tree-lined roads, the trunks painted white so that the route would be visible in the dark, since there were no cats' eyes. The dangers of travelling at night in Romania were many. Apart from the many potholes, turning a corner could lead to a collision with a farmer sleeping in his horse-drawn cart.

On passing into Hungary, we remembered just in time that we had hidden our Bibles and tapes, and stopped to reclaim them. Roger and I ventured quickly into the woods, which were known to be inhabited by bears and wolves, but could not find our possessions. We could not believe it, and feared the worst – that the authorities had found and confiscated them. We tried again, and discovered them under a pile of soil, leaves and twigs.

It was quite beautiful driving through the early hours of the morning in Hungary, watching the sun rise over fields of sunflowers, and passing through the capital city as it began to stir at the dawning of a new day. The early-morning mist hung over the Danube as we crossed one of the many bridges and bade farewell to one of the most beautiful cities in Europe.

A few weeks later Ruth and I met Roger and Doreen to talk over our trip. We felt a burden to help our brothers and sisters in Hungary and Romania, and decided to appeal to Spurgeon's College students for aid, which we planned to send by truck to a base in Austria. Over the next year we continued to raise funds, and several convoys went from the UK to our contacts in Hungary, from where it was transported to Romania slowly but inconspicuously.

Because the boundary between Hungary and Romania had been redrawn in 1925, a number of people living in the town of Debrecen on the Hungarian-Romanian border had family in Romania, and were able to travel freely and frequently between these two countries. It was impossible to drive aid into Romania, because President Ceaucescu maintained there was no need; he wanted Romanians to believe that their nation was one of the most prosperous in Europe, without need of assistance from the West.

The pastor of the Baptist church in Debrecen, who was known to us, kept our aid in the church's basement and would arrange for those of his church members who had dual nationality to carry a jar of coffee, a bag of flour, a hot-water bottle or shoes in the basket of their bicycles underneath the vegetables or flowers they had grown themselves. This team of 'supergrannies', aged between fifty and eighty, would cycle merrily across the border into Romania and share the goods with desperately needy families and churches. It often took around three months to get the whole three-ton truckful of aid over the border in this way. The system continued until the fall of Ceaucescu in December 1989.

1989: Oradea and Cluj

In the summer of 1989 I took a coach-load of Baptists old and young to the European Baptist Federation in Budapest, at which Billy Graham was due to preach. When we arrived, I met up with the drivers of one of our aid trucks and went on with some aid to Debrecen, travelling with a college friend, Paul Grinyer, and two fellow Baptists, Jo Thomson and Kathryn Peake.

A shock awaited us. We discovered that our friend, the pastor of the church where the aid was stored, had died suddenly of a heart attack. We spent the day off-loading the latest truck and comforting the church members. The next day we loaded up our own car and set off with aid for Romania.

I had a list of addresses which I had hidden in my suitcase between my clothes. We had hoped that, as our party consisted of two men and two women, we would not arouse too much suspicion. But our car was completely searched, and the suitcase containing the addresses of Christians was confiscated.

Our destination was the Second Baptist Church of Oradea, the largest single Baptist church in Europe, with three thousand members. A service was in progress when we arrived, and two thousand people were sitting outside listening to it on the PA system. The crowd had to be seen to be believed. This was indeed a welcome spiritual oasis of singing and prayer in those dark days of Communism.

We were spotted and invited into the church, which was absolutely packed. A sea of three thousand faces looked at us as we were ushered on to the platform behind the pulpit where a pastor was preaching. We stuck out like a sore thumb and simply wanted to sit and listen in the background, but we were expected to bring a greeting from the West. The service lasted several hours, with wonderful Romanian singing, tremendous preaching and an amazing time of prayer. It was a foretaste of heaven. Though we could not understand the Romanian language, we knew that we were all one in Christ Jesus, because of his sacrifice on the cross which achieved salvation for all who trust in him as Lord and Saviour.

After the service we were ushered into the minister's vestry, where we were greeted by the Rev. Paul Negrut, the associate minister. Before we could speak, Paul put his fingers to his lips to indicate that we should be silent. The curtains were drawn, the telephone was taken off the hook and put under a cushion, a radio was turned on and deacons were staged around the church as lookouts. We asked whether either Paul or his senior pastor, Dr Nic, would be attending the Congress in Budapest, but were amazed to discover that no visas were being issued to Romanian Christians until after the Congress had finished. As I had a video camera with me, I asked Paul if he would be willing to tape a message for Billy Graham, which we then filmed in secret. Paul said on the tape: 'Although we are not able to be with you since the authorities are not allowing us to come out of Romania, we are with you in spirit and in prayer, and hope that you have a great conference, and that one day soon we may be free to share with our brothers and sisters in the West.' Little did he know that less than six months later, this would indeed be possible.

After that meeting, we were given coffee and cake, and shared out some money that we had taken. We left some gifts with a young doctor, his pregnant wife and their young daughter. This doctor, one of the leaders of the church, had requested specific medicines for his village clinic, and these we were able to deliver. He was delighted with what we had brought him, since he had very limited resources, and had to cover a twenty-five-mile radius on his bicycle as he sought to bring comfort and relief to those in the villages around his home.

From Oradea we travelled to Cluj, catching up with John and Monica Achim, and from there to Alba Iulia to deliver medicines to Monica's sister and the Christian woman, a doctor, with whom she shared her flat. This woman was helping Gypsy children in the area. She told us about the Gypsy church that had been established, and how many were coming to know Christ even in the face of persecution and hardship.

While with these two women, we had a time of prayer, but sensed the ever-present need to be secretive. We talked in hushed tones so that the neighbours would not hear our western voices and contact the Securitate. Many Romanians were encouraged to snoop and to shop their neighbours for not working, not paying their taxes, and having westerners in their home. As a reward for their loyalty to Ceaucescu and the nation, they would be given more food and clothing vouchers. Ceaucescu also had a plan of 'systemization', by which he aimed to destroy villages and place residents in tower blocks, where they could be controlled more easily. These were the pressures Christians were having to live under day by day.

A divine intervention

Our next stop was Hateg, where we were to meet with a pastor we knew. On the way, we had to pass through Hunedoara, a town near a sulphur factory. We could not believe our eyes as we saw houses and trees covered in orange dust. Children in shorts were playing football barefoot, covered from head to toe in orange. Our medicines would help the many suffering from asthma, other bronchial diseases, and blood poisoning.

As we drove towards Hateg, we passed a military camp right on the edge of the town. Our brand new hired red Escort was highly conspicuous, and we were in two minds whether or not to stop. But the need for the medicines to be delivered compelled us to continue to seek the pastor out, not least because his own health was failing. Though only thirty years of age, he suffered from a heart condition.

We did not have an address, only his name and telephone number. While three of us waited in the car, Paul went to make the telephone call. Ten minutes later he returned, saying there was just a Romanian voice on the other end and it obviously wasn't anything to do with a Baptist church or pastor. We sent Paul back to try again, because the phone number was all we had to go on. We waited patiently in the car in the midday sunshine. After an hour, Paul had still not returned and we became quite concerned.

Later, we learned that as Paul was making the call, a burly six-foot-three Romanian had suddenly grabbed him and marched him down the street, weaving his way through numerous tower blocks, with Paul remonstrating and fearing that he had been grabbed by the Securitate. The man led Paul into a block of flats and up to the tenth floor, where he knocked on a door. Who should greet Paul but the very pastor we had come to meet! It turned out that the telephone number we had was incorrect and we could never have found him by ringing it. The burly Romanian had been sitting in a barber's shop across the road from where Paul was making the telephone call. He felt prompted by the Holy Spirit to take Paul to his pastor, though he was a young Christian and spoke no English. This incident encouraged our faith and affirmed that where God guides, he certainly provides.

We spent a too-brief thirty minutes with the pastor, his wife and family, and were able to hand over the medicines and pray with them, before we went on our way. We shall never forget the miraculous intervention which brought us to them.

We drove through various villages towards the city of Arad. *En route* we stopped at one village where we met a Christian man who did not speak English but who welcomed us into his home, gave us a drink and some fruit, and provided fresh, cool water from the well in his garden. After much sign language between us, he cried with delight when he found out that we were Christians, and we discovered that he was lay pastor of a Baptist church in the village.

In Arad we met up with another pastor to deliver aid. He was waiting for us and bade us enter his flat, like Paul Negrut, with a finger to his lips, warning us to be silent. The telephone was disconnected, the radio was switched on and the blinds were drawn, and we talked about all that God was doing in his town. He was a very experienced and outspoken pastor, under whom the church had grown rapidly and spread out into several plants. The previous Sunday they had baptized forty-four members in the local river. He showed us pictures and asked us to take them home with us to show other Christians in the West so that they might pray for the church and these new converts. He was being hounded and persecuted severely by the authorities because of his outspokenness against the Ceaucescu regime, and his flat was being watched. We ourselves had to be careful of the police as we left.

After this meeting we left Romania, but not without difficulty. At the border we were all body-searched, and our car was inspected thoroughly. Fortunately, we had hidden the video message for Billy Graham from Paul Negrut. Once back at the

European Baptist Federation Congress, we were able to pass the tape to Dr Graham personally.

The remaining few days went exceedingly well, with Christians from East and West enjoying wonderful fellowship. The climax of the congress was the big crusade meeting in the Nep stadium, a hundred thousand squeezing into an area designed for sixty thousand. They sat on every inch of the playing field, listening to a five-hundred-strong Hungarian choir, and the testimony and beautiful singing of paraplegic Joni Eareckson Tada, as well as Billy Graham's preaching. It was very moving to see over fifteen hundred people go forward to accept Jesus Christ as their Lord and Saviour.

The fall of Ceaucescu

Later that year, on 16 and 17 December, Romanian demonstrators were shot in Timisoara. As a result, more demonstrations followed all over the country. Television pictures on 21 December showed Ceaucescu trying to calm the marauding crowds from his presidential balcony, but with little success. He was shouted down, and on the following day the army joined the rebels. Ceaucescu fled from the presidential palace in his private helicopter (reputedly with US $1 billion) but he was arrested at the airport on his way out of the country. He and his wife were imprisoned. On 23 December the National Salvation Front took control of Romania, and on Christmas Day, the seventy-two-year-old Ceaucescu and his wife Elena faced a firing squad and were shot.

It later transpired that the top forty political positions in Romania had been filled by members of Ceaucescu's immediate family. While peasants struggled to find sufficient food for their families, the Ceaucescus had enjoyed a lavish lifestyle in over a dozen homes around the country, complete with indoor jacuzzis, swimming pools, marbled bathrooms, gold taps, and servants. Luxury food and drink, such as caviar and champagne, had been flown in from Switzerland at the whim of the family.

KEY EVENTS IN EASTERN EUROPE, 1989-90

1989

4 June	Partial free elections in Poland won by Solidarity
24 August	Mazowiecki becomes the first non-Communist Prime Minister of Poland
11 September	Hungary opens its borders to East Germans fleeing to Austria
18 October	East German leader, Erich Honecker, resigns
23 October	New Hungarian Republic declared
8 November	Berlin Wall collapses; thousands cross to the West
10 November	Zhibkov deposed in Bulgaria
17 November	Demonstrations in Prague violently suppressed
24 November	Czechoslovakian government resigns
10 December	Non-Communist government sworn in in Czechoslovakia
11 December	Communist Party proposes a multi-party system in Bulgaria
16–17 December	Romanian demonstrators killed in Timisoara
21 December	Crowds shout down Ceaucescu in Romania
22 December	Romanian army joins rebels; Ceaucescu flees and is captured

23 December	National Salvation Front takes charge of Romania
25 December	Ceaucescu and his wife Elena shot
30 December	Vaclav Havel elected president of Czechoslovakia

1990

18 March	Free elections in East Germany won by Allies for Germany (48%), the former Communist Party
25 March/8 April	Free elections in Hungary won by Democratic Forum (42%), the former Communist Party
20 May	Disputed elections in Romania won by National Salvation Front (66%). No opposition party awarded more than 7%
8 June	Free elections in Czechoslovakia won by Civic Forum
10/17 June	Free elections in Bulgaria won by Socialist Party (46%); Union of Democratic Forces gained 37%

(Source: *Conscience and Captivity* by Janice Broun)

5

ROMANIAN RELIEF,
1990-91

In January I was asked by the *Croydon Advertiser*, which had featured some of my convoy work, to return to Romania with a reporter and photographer to capture, over a long weekend, the changes that had taken place in the brief period since Ceaucescu's downfall. Over the next few weeks, I organized a truck of aid to go overland and meet us there.

We met them at the border near Oradea, where the scene that greeted our eyes was unbelievable when compared with our previous experience at the border. On this cold day at the end of January, burly guards in thick military coats welcomed with open arms the hundreds of trucks filled with food, clothes and medicines which were queuing to enter Romania at the dawn of a new day for this nation. On arrival, all trucks were put under military guard to prevent any pilfering.

In the hotel in Oradea where we spent the night, the welcome was the same. Where once it had been quiet, sombre and uninviting, now it was packed with truck drivers, volunteers and aid workers who gave it a sort of festival atmosphere. The hotel staff could not do enough for us all. It was also a time of wonderful fellowship as we discovered Christian representatives from Sweden, America, France, Germany and Spain. It was a historic time, and wonderful to be part of it.

The next day we headed for Cluj, delivering aid to villages on the way. In Cluj we dropped off aid at the Manastur Baptist Church, where I had preached eighteen months before. It had now been given permission to extend, a privilege church members had been seeking for twenty-five years, during which time it was allowed only to expand its walls ten feet in either direction and to add a large basement for use as a sports hall and Sunday-school classroom. We stored the aid there.

Worse than Dracula

We met with a number of Christian doctors, nurses and pharmacists, who had recently opened a Christian pharmacy in Cluj. Here they not only treated those who were ill, but gave all comers a New Testament.

We were asked by some of the doctors if we would take some of our aid to an orphanage in a small mountain village just outside the town. We agreed, and left that evening in the snow and complete darkness. Halfway up the mountain, we turned into a side road, where the fog that descended with the night became so dense that we could hardly see where we were going. Our seven-and-a-half-ton truck took up virtually the whole of the narrow lane, and some of us had to get out to make sure that it did not get stuck.

We eventually arrived at some big iron gates in a stone wall, the mist swirling about them – a scene reminiscent of Dracula's castle in Bram Stoker's novel. The long, narrow drive leading up to the grey, crumbling orphanage revealed no sign of life whatsoever. We wondered whether we had come to the right place, or whether it had been closed down and the children sent away.

Two of our party went off to investigate, returning after about twenty minutes to beckon us in. We made our way down the stone steps of this apparently deserted building into a basement room. As we opened the door, we could not believe the scene that greeted our eyes. Around three hundred boys aged between four and twelve were huddled together, about to have their evening meal. The temperature outside had fallen to –15°C, and the boys gathered around the tables in coats, gloves, hats and scarves, trying to keep warm. There was no heating in the building. Their evening meal consisted of one raw onion, a cup of cold water and a slice of stale bread. There were no bowls, no plates, no knives, and no forks. They ate off the cracked, dirty and damaged tables. The only people looking after them were three old ladies from the nearby village. This was the legacy of Ceaucescu's regime.

The Dickensian scene before us left us speechless with shock. We could not believe that such deprivation existed in modern Europe, just a couple of hours' flight from London. This was a result of Ceaucescu's policy that every woman between the ages of sixteen and forty should have six children. Failure to do so meant heavy taxes. But the poverty of many families meant that they could afford to feed only two or three of their children. The others were handed over to the orphanage, although they were not orphans. They had parents, but those parents were unable to care for them and genuinely believed that they stood a better chance of survival if they were fed and housed in a state institution.

We were shown around and found that there were no carpets, no glass in some of the windows, no toys, no pictures on the walls, nothing to indicate that these children were having a happy childhood. In the bedrooms there were only metal beds with soiled mattresses and a heap of blankets. In a number of rooms we found children huddling in bed, wearing coats and gloves. Many of them suffered from mental disorders or were physically disabled.

In one room we discovered many children who were unable to walk. These were called 'crawlers'. The typical mother of these children had usually had six children, but found herself pregnant again, and attempted an abortion on herself. (Under Ceaucescu, contraception and abortion were banned.) This would often go badly wrong and result in the child being born disabled, perhaps without arms or legs, or deaf, mute, blind or brain-damaged. Ceaucescu believed that the greater the population of Romania, the greater the country's power in the world forum. But he succeeded only in creating sheer misery for parents and for the children who were living in the nightmare we now saw before us.

The smell in the orphanage was unbelievable. From time to time we had to go outside for a breath of fresh air, despite the fact that it was a freezing February night. We off-loaded our aid into the big kitchens: sugar, flour, oil, clothes, sweets and belated

Christmas presents, which were received gratefully. As we walked around the dark, dismal orphanage, a place more reminiscent of a prison than a home for children, we wondered why there were no girls. The orphanage authorities would not comment, but we understood from the church leaders who were with us that Ceaucescu had been more interested in male children who would grow to serve the nation in the Securitate or the army. It was understood that many baby girls were either left to die or were killed.

We met other children, many of whom had no shoes, despite the wintry conditions. They were walking around in socks. At the back of the orphanage, however, we discovered several wooden sheds which turned out to be miniature shoe factories. The children would make shoes there, which they would then hawk around the mountain villages, selling them for a pittance so that the orphanage authorities could buy them food. State support was negligible.

Often such orphanages were hidden from the view of ordinary Romanians, and, indeed, the Romanian Christians who were with us had not realized until a few weeks before that such a place existed. It was only after the fall of Ceaucescu that they were able to enter the premises and discover the appalling horror hiding there.

Our long drive back to Cluj was made in silence as we tried and failed to come to terms with what we had seen. Nothing had prepared us for it. Our reactions swung between disbelief, anger, and compassion for the children. We all undertook to return and improve the conditions they were living in, and to assist with their medical difficulties.

Romania: 'hot news'

The next day we were taken to a hospital to deliver some of the goods we had brought. We talked with the doctors and made a list of medicines and equipment that were desperately needed. The matron rallied together a group of twenty-four children to help us unload the trucks; they were patients undergoing treatment for a variety of diseases. On this cold Saturday morning, in temperatures of $-10°C$, they were dressed only in pyjamas, slippers and dressing-gowns as they formed a chain down which we passed food, clothes and medicines.

As we were unloading, two porters carried the dead body of a man on a stretcher from a ward to the mortuary in full view of fellow patients looking out of the windows. This was the reality of having insufficient medicines, medical equipment and staff.

That afternoon we had a tour of Cluj, where eighteen months earlier I had walked with my wife and child. Now there were shrines on every street corner to those who had lost their lives in the revolution just six weeks ago. The buildings were liberally peppered with bullet holes, a lasting legacy of the conflict. Pictures of young men who had died were plastered on the walls of the streets, and small white candles burned in rusty metal tins on window ledges where somebody's dear son had died for the sake of freedom. Crosses made out of laurel branches, and wreaths, adorned every corner of the main square, which had obviously been the setting of a fierce battle for several weeks. Many inhabitants of Cluj were still wandering around in a state of euphoria over the freedom they had won, but also in shock at the cost with which it had been gained – the lives of many idealistic students who had fought a brave battle against well-armed Securitate troops. As we wandered into the Orthodox cathedral of St Michael, special prayers and sombre services were being said for those who had lost loved ones.

That evening we returned to the home of John and Monica Achim, whom I had visited in 1988. Monica graphically described how she had been in the market in the town square as soldiers began to fire on unarmed students demonstrating there. Bullets were flying everywhere, she said; people were screaming and running; children and students lay bleeding and dying all over the square. With tears in her eyes and a quivering voice, Monica related how she was encouraging a student to run away, but he refused, choosing to stand and fight for freedom. Thirty seconds later a bullet went straight through his head. Part of his brains splattered on to Monica's coat. She cradled the dying eighteen-year-old boy in her arms in the centre of Cluj as fear, chaos and panic reigned around them. She could not believe that this was no invading army, but Romanian soldiers killing Romanian citizens. Similar scenes were played out in Timisoara, Arad, Oradea, Brasov and Bucharest, in a week of uncertainty that was to shape the future of Romania and other Eastern European countries for years to come.

The next morning we went to the local Baptist church for the morning service, where our atheistic newspaper reporter was amazed at how, on this cold February morning, hundreds of people packed into the church to worship God and a further hundred stood outside as the fine, powdery snow fell. They stood for three hours as they prayed, worshipped and listened to God's Word.

On the flight on the way home, I got talking to a man who turned out to be a programme director for a London radio station. He invited me on to a show the next day to share with listeners what I had experienced on this trip. Romania was 'hot news' at that moment. As a result of that interview, I was filmed by the BBC and recordings of our visit were shown on the local evening news. The response to these broadcasts could not be measured. They were among the first reports on the Romanian orphanages to be seen on British television. At one point we were receiving over fifty phone calls a day, and sacks of aid were being delivered to our door. Eventually, our garage was full as well. The next Sunday I was unable to get to my house after church services as cars lined up to deliver more food, clothes and medicines. We started filling up the old air-raid shelter at church, and spent the rest of the day unloading what people had brought.

Over the next few days a number of local Christians began to sort through what had been donated, and a local hotelier offered his ballroom as a storage area. On the great dance floor, beneath the chandeliers and glitter balls, piles of shoes and clothes thirty feet high were arranged, sorted and sent for washing and repair, before being sent out to Romania. We were amazed and saddened at the appalling condition of some of the goods that were given to us, many tons of which were fit only for burning or for use as rags. We agreed only to send items that we would be willing to wear ourselves or to put on our own children's backs. Several dozen volunteers from local churches helped every evening. It was a truly significant joint project.

In addition to clothes, I received telephone calls from a meat company offering ten tons of corned beef, a light-bulb company offering ten thousand bulbs, an airline offering five hundred stewarding uniforms which had been printed with the wrong logo, a hospital offering medical goods and baby clothes, and a doctor offering one million paracetamol tablets. We had to send two seven-and-a-half-ton trucks to pick them up; there was probably enough paracetamol there to cure every Romanian headache for a month, if not longer.

With the money that was donated we were able to purchase pharmaceutical medicines from the charity ECHO (Equipping Charity Hospitals Overseas). The staff there were extremely helpful, providing thousands of pounds'-worth of necessary medicines and equipment.

It was vital that our aid went through recognized and registered churches. It had to be listed clearly and easily accounted for to prevent it from slipping on to the black market, which at that time was making a few individuals extremely rich. This factor put some charitable organizations off giving aid to the needy orphans of Romania and hindered the contribution of funds to some others.

The frequent media reports on the situation in Romania, and the fact that the country was a mere two or three days' drive across Europe, meant that many organizations travelled there with aid. It seemed at that time as if all roads led to Romania. Unfortunately, many of the visitors had had no previous contact with any Romanians. They would simply find an orphanage, drive up, drop off their load at the front door (much to the delight of the orphanage manager), turn round and go back to the UK. The manager and staff would give some of this aid to the children, but much of it would go out of the back door to their own families or be sold on the black market to make up for the wages they had not received for a year.

July 1990: church-building

That summer I returned to Romania with four colleagues to see how our aid programme was developing. We were met by Dr Vasile Talpos, a small, plumpish man in his early fifties with receding grey hair, who was tremendously active not only as Principal of the Baptist seminary, but also as minister of Hope Baptist Church in Bucharest, a church of three hundred members. As we walked around the city together that evening, we saw the marks of the revolution (as we had done in Cluj), but it was good, too, to witness a new Christian bookshop that had opened in the shadow of Ceaucescu's palace. Crowds of people flocked to the shop, where Bibles, tracts, posters and music tapes, all of which had been banned under the old regime, were now for sale.

We walked down the main avenue built by Ceaucescu: a road about one and a half miles long and five hundred yards wide, leading from the centre of the capital to the ruler's palace, and cutting a swathe through the heart of some of the oldest Orthodox church buildings in Romania.

The building of the palace and its grandiose approach had attracted tremendous criticism from around the world. The palace, known to Romanians as the White House, contains three thousand rooms and was allegedly built by Romanians who were expected to work for no pay. A number of the builders died in the attempt, or were killed by the Securitate for constructing some of the building incorrectly. Local Christians also point out that beneath the palace, the largest building in Europe, Ceaucescu built a labyrinth which stretches beneath the whole of Bucharest, to enable him to control every area of the nation's life: finance, commerce, politics. Securitate officials would pop up in the oddest of places across the city and then disappear. It was only after the fall of Ceaucescu that these tunnels were discovered. An order was given to seal them off.

While we were in Romania, we understood that government officials were occupying the palace, but that it might be sold to an American organization to be turned into one of the largest hotels in the world. Many Romanians, however, were calling for its destruction.

From Bucharest we moved to Iasi, where we were to preach in a local church. We arrived at our destination to find about fifty church members, ranging from small children to grandparents, busy mixing concrete and cement and knocking down walls to extend the building. Under their new-found freedom, they had had no difficulty in obtaining permission to do this.

That evening we enjoyed good Romanian hospitality before attending a packed meeting in the basement of the church. For three hours a continual torrent of loud prayers flowed, mixed with wonderful worship and a response to God's Word which saw a number of people dedicate their hearts to the Lord.

The following day we were taken to look at another church

which had been planted a few weeks previously in a home on the far side of Iasi. There, too, members were hard at work, converting some outbuildings into a Sunday-school room. The new church could seat about seventy people comfortably, and the Sunday school would accommodate about two hundred children. It was wonderful to see how the Romanian believers, who had worked hard all week in their regular jobs, gave their evenings and weekends to the church for no reward save that of making God known in their nation. The older women provided meals all day as the men, younger women and children sawed and nailed wood, mixed cement, laid bricks, rewired, and fixed doors and windows. You name it, we saw them doing it.

That afternoon we looked around Iasi, the former Orthodox capital of Romania, which has a delightful park with a number of statues and a wonderful view over the countryside. Later we drove to a town called Piatra-Neamt. There we met an energetic young pastor called Marin, a married man with several young children, who, like most pastors, had not just one church to minister to, but about ten. He was pioneering work in a further three towns and villages in the area. The people of God were working tirelessly to make the most of their new-found freedom, uncertain how long it would last. We visited an area near Lake Bicaz where foundations for a new church had been dug and the wood for the roof got together. The church members were now praying for sufficient resources to buy bricks and mortar with which to build.

'Amen!' said the cow

Pastor Marin took us to a beautiful mountain area with a spectacular gorge, near to Lake Rosu, an area popular with Romanians for holidays. After this excursion we went up to Suceava, in the farthest north-east corner of the country, to meet Pastor Dan Bougarnou and preach in his church the next day. We had to be up at seven o'clock to attend the first service at nine in a small village church, which was really an old lady's home some ten miles north of the town. Around a hundred people crammed into this house for a four-hour service, which included three baptisms. The candidates, in their sixties, seventies and eighties, were baptized in a big cast-iron tank that had been brought in specially from a local farm. It was a fascinating experience, and I felt privileged to be able to preach to this church. Halfway through my sermon, a cow popped its head in at the doorway and mooed. I commented that the cow was saying 'Amen!' to my words, a remark which was well received.

After the service, tables and benches were lined up in the farmyard which surrounded the old lady's home, and thirty or forty people sat down to lunch. The fellowship continued all day until we had to leave for a church in the town.

At that evening service, a number of young people came forward to give their lives to the Lord. There was tremendous spiritual fervour and a great interest in God and Christian spirituality. Pastor Dan, a well-respected minister, had a powerful vision for Suceava, and was embarking upon the building of a new Baptist church, complete with a seminary to train up more pastors, of whom there was a great dearth. Under Ceaucescu, only six students had been allowed to train at the Baptist seminary each year. There were fifteen hundred Baptist churches in Romania, with something like two hundred and fifty pastors, most of whom were aged between fifty and eighty. Ceaucescu sought to crush Christianity simply by making it difficult to train leaders, but in fact the church grew under persecution and now there was a need to train as many pastors as possible. At that time just £10 or £15 a month was all that was required to fund a pastor and his family in their ministry.

The following day we were driven along the beautiful mountain road from Suceava to Cluj, a journey of about four hours. We stopped at Dracula's castle in a spectacular forest area for lunch, and while we were eating we got talking to members of the Romanian national basketball team, who had turned up at the same restaurant. They asked us why we had come to Romania, and we told them that we were British Christians seeking to encourage the Romanian church. At the end of a lengthy conversation, some of the young men asked us to pray with them, and we saw them commit their lives to Christ. Such an encounter would not have been possible less than a year previously, when Ceaucescu was still in power.

Orphanage transformed!

Back in Cluj, we again visited the Manastur Baptist Church, where the new building was progressing rapidly. We again visited the orphanage, and this time it was a great joy to find a remarkable difference in the condition of both the orphanage and the children themselves. There were now carpets and heating, glass in the windows, pictures on the walls, painted murals of Disney characters, toys, and proper nurses caring for the children. When we had last seen them in February, they had looked gaunt and near to death, but now, in July, they were the picture of health. Their faces were fuller, they were cleaner, and they were more responsive as a result of the love and attention they were receiving from their new Romanian doctors and nurses. While there, we met a team of twenty or so British young people who had given three weeks of their summer holiday to improve conditions at the orphanage, together with other volunteers from around Europe. They had painted the beautiful murals on the walls, redecorated bedrooms, fitted windows, fixed beds and, most of all, spent time playing and working with the children and cuddling them.

Some of the children had been able to return to their families, but many had not, because their families were still unable to feed and care for them. The truth was that many of the children in the orphanages were now better looked after than children at home, and this was leading to some resentment in the local communities.

We spent time talking with the local mayor and officials, and were amazed to learn that the high walls and fences surrounding the orphanage, which once prevented the children from escaping, were now retained to keep people out and prevent them from stealing the aid which arrived almost daily from the West. After these talks, we decided to set up a community clinic at the orphanage as a place where all the local families could receive treatment, food, clothes and shoes. In this way, aid could be shared with the whole area, and the orphanage would cease to be an island of rich resources surrounded by a sea of poverty.

In Cluj itself, a lighter, brighter atmosphere greeted us in summer compared to February. New doors of opportunity were opening, and it was important for Christians to be sensitive to the needs of the whole nation rather than to small groups of hospitals, orphanages or churches. It was disappointing, however, to see more negative western influences taking hold. A number of people were now unemployed and had taken to drink and drugs. Pornography was sweeping the nation, and there had been a rapid increase in violence, prostitution and crime. We were told that some of the major crime committed was not Mafia-controlled, as in other countries, but was carried out by former members of the Securitate. Having once been privy to information, they were now using their contacts, influence and weapons for their own personal ends, and turning to such enterprises as drug-trafficking, importing alcohol, and establishing protection rackets.

Before returning home, I met church leaders and was invited to bring a team of students to evangelize with the churches just before Christmas. From Cluj we returned to Bucharest, completing our triangular tour of the country.

December 1990: fog and fellowship

By December I had gathered together a group of twenty fellow students from Spurgeon's College, and a seven-and-a-half-ton truck of aid had been organized, which would travel overland and meet us in Bucharest. The truck had been filled with donations from members of the college, and from the churches with which they had contact; and the seven tons' worth we had asked for had become twenty-one tons. The college games room, located in a mobile cabin adjacent to the main college buildings, was used as a storeroom.

On 10 December our team flew to Bucharest, enjoying a time of fellowship during the flight in a plane half-filled with Christian aid workers.

In Bucharest, we met fellow students, shared a meal and enjoyed some wonderful singing from the student choir, before bedding down on the lecture-room floors. The next morning, we led a time of worship in the college chapel, and then unloaded the overhead projectors, theological books, English-language tapes, Hebrew and Greek textbooks, keyboard, PA system, Bibles, acetates, pens, paper and food, which we had brought with us.

We then made our way to the railway station and headed for Ploesti, where the Baptist minister and his wife welcomed all twenty of us into their home for lunch, without any sense of panic or difficulty whatsoever. From there we went to the mountain town of Brasov, known for its wonderful skiing. We met a number of Christians, who treated us to a sightseeing tour of their historic city, which included a cable-car ride up to a mountain top. It was like a Christmas wonderland, with trees encased in sparkling frost and the sun trying to burst through the winter fog.

We also had a guided tour of the Black Cathedral in Brasov's town centre, built between 1384 and 1477 and still used today by German Lutherans. At the local Baptist church, we preached and sang in a midweek service to a congregation of around five hundred in a building complete with enormous chandeliers suspended thirty feet from the high ceiling above on great chains. After the service, we were all taken in twos or threes to various homes for dinner and an overnight stay, an experience which gave us an insight into the difficulties many Romanians were facing. We off-loaded further aid at the church the next day, before beginning the next leg of our journey on a meandering mountain road through freezing fog and snow to Tirgu-Mures.

We broke our difficult journey in Sighisoara, a perfectly preserved medieval town. No fewer than eleven towers remained on the town's intact walls, embracing the sloping cobbled streets lined with sixteenth-century burgher houses and untouched churches. This Transylvanian region was the birthplace and homeland of Prince Vlad Tepes, the ruling prince of Wallachia from 1456 to 1462, who led a resistance to the expanding Ottoman empire. He was known as 'the Impaler', from his habit of impaling the heads of slain Turkish foes on stakes. This may seem extreme, but Transylvania has had a tumultuous past. Bram Stoker's character, Count Dracula, was based upon Vlad Tepes.

Less gruesome has been the work of German Baptists in this area. Sent by the famous German evangelist J. G. Oncken, one Mr Weigl, an ironmaster and member of a Baptist church in Berlin, came to Bucharest to find work in 1862. He soon gathered a small group of believers around him and founded a church. Part of Oncken's strategy was to send out young Baptist pioneers to promote the Baptist cause in other countries. His notable motto was, 'Every Baptist a missionary'. In 1872, the colporteur J. Hammerschmidt became the new church's pastor, and was supported by the German Bible Society. The church grew, but a constant stream of emigrants to the United States did not help the Baptist cause in Romania. After fifty years' labour, the Bucharest church had just eighty-seven members among a population of over forty thousand German-speakers. For twenty-five years (1880 to 1905), Hammerschmidt continued his work. He was replaced by the Rev. Berg Schlipf, who travelled to fellow Germans scattered around the land. He had two assistants, who sold over six thousand Bibles each year, and together they established churches in the Black Sea area.

The first Hungarian Baptist church was established in Salonta in 1871, and concentrated mainly on the central and northern parts of Romania, leaving the east to the Russians and the centre and the capital to the Germans. It was estimated that in 1910, there were just two hundred Romanian-speaking Baptists. Today there are two hundred thousand.

We visited a German Baptist Church to off-load some equipment on our way to Tirgu-Mures, where we shared at a church service and again spent the night in members' homes. A few weeks previously we had read in the news of fighting and shootings in the town, a conflict between Romanians and Hungarians, sparked off by a Hungarian baker who put a sign in his window saying that he would not sell to Romanians. As we noted earlier, Hungarians consider this region as their rightful land, because before 1928 it formed part of Hungary.

Opposition from the Orthodox

We heard from the Tirgu-Mures Baptist pastor that the Jehovah's Witnesses were making strong inroads into the nearby mountain villages and that Mormons had sent teams of evangelists, as had the 'Moonies'. Transcendental Meditation and yoga were also taking hold. The battle for the heart and soul of Romania was certainly on, and it was sobering to hear the cry of Romanian Christians that the present opportunity to strengthen the church should be taken. They feared that if the gospel were not proclaimed and opportunities for people to turn to Christ were not provided, many Romanians would be lost to cults. Evangelical churches were also experiencing opposition from the national Orthodox Church, as its members defected from the latter to the former. Orthodoxy was seeking and gaining support from the government in its role as state church, a move which threw into doubt the future of liberty for all Christians. Politicians were linking evangelicals and cults as parts of one movement, tarring them all with the same brush. The Baptist Union and the Evangelical Alliance were working to clarify the great differences between the Baptist Church and these new religious movements.

The following morning we took some aid to an orphanage. As we made our way up a very muddy and snowy track, the weight of the truck's contents made it sink into the mud up to its axle. As we attempted to dig it out, we prayed that the Lord would help us. Just then a massive Romanian army pick-up truck came round the corner. Its wheels were six feet high. After I had talked with the driver in sign language, he connected our truck to his and effortlessly pulled it out.

We were then able to take the aid to the orphanage at the top of the hill and play a while with the children, before returning to the pastor's home, where a meal of soup, rice and meat was again served to twenty hungry students without any fuss or bother. That afternoon we continued our journey to Cluj, winding our way through snow-covered mountain villages, and witnessing the extraordinary sight of bloated pig carcasses lying on their backs, surrounded by farmers who were trying to remove the trotters with blow-torches. Our Romanian friends told us that this was the pig-killing season. Christmas was just a week away, and the pigs would be slaughtered, their trotters and meat being used to make sausages and soup to keep for the harsh winter months ahead.

In Cluj, we separated to go to different churches in the area, at which we would preach and assist in services. As my colleague Andy Gore preached at the church we attended, his translator's Romanian sentences seemed long when Andy's were short, and short when Andy's were long. Afterwards, we good-humouredly enquired whether he had been preaching the same sermon. He smiled and answered quietly, 'You will never know.' Later he joked that he had been correcting Andy's theology as well as giving an interpretation.

The next day, our team was reunited, and we shared accounts of our different Sundays. Two students, who had gone to a very remote mountain area to preach in several Pentecostal churches, had seen an amazing response as people committed their lives to Christ and many healings took place. Similar reports challenged, stimulated and encouraged our students as they contemplated the spiritual hunger which caused many Romanians to respond to the gospel.

We heard that morning that our plane back to Bucharest had been cancelled, so we boarded a train from Cluj for an eight-hour journey to the capital. The train was without heating or lighting. The temperature was −10°C and the train never moved faster than around thirty miles an hour. As the journey progressed, the weary students huddled in the compartments and shared how much God had encouraged them through their previous day's preaching. We had several hundred tracts with us, and the team began to evangelize their fellow travellers. I remember vividly sharing the gospel with a Romanian woman of twenty-one, who had a very difficult relationship with a violent boyfriend, and who was keen to know more about being a Christian. As a result of this encounter, she wrote to me for several years afterwards, telling me of improvements in her situation and her involvement with a church in Bucharest.

God provides VIP treatment

We were due to leave Bucharest at 10am on 17 December, one year to the day since the start of the revolution. Arriving at the airport, we discovered that strikes were occurring all across the country in an expression of disappointment at the new government's inability to implement reforms and increase prosperity. Teachers were on strike, train operators were on strike, and now airport staff were walking out, too. As we waited in the unheated airport lounge, we learnt that the air-traffic controllers would walk out at five o'clock and that there would be no flights from the airport until the new year. We were encouraged to find alternative arrangements for getting back to England. I made a number of frantic telephone calls to the Baptist seminary and talked to any official I could find who understood English.

While we were waiting, we met a number of English, German, and American nurses and others travelling home for Christmas, including orphanage workers and parents who had adopted month-old babies.

As I walked around the airport I discovered an empty, carpeted VIP lounge with comfortable seats and curtains, which was far warmer than the draughty concourse where the temperature was –5°C. (Outside it was –15°C.) We could not see any planes on the runway, as it was obscured by freezing fog and a blizzard. I asked one of the officials if we could use the VIP lounge. He responded that it was really only for ambassadors and high-ranking officials. I explained to him that I was an ambassador. He looked somewhat surprised and asked which king I served. I told him that I served King Jesus, as did the rest of the team, and that therefore we should be allowed to use these facilities. After a few moments of pondering and negotiation with his colleagues, he allowed us all into the VIP lounge, much to our relief.

Several more hours of discussion and negotiation took place. It was looking less and less likely that we would get home in time for Christmas. Some of our students had recently married, and were extremely worried. We had tried everything else; all that remained to do was to pray. A few moments after we had gathered together for prayer, I was waved over to an official's desk. He explained to me that a plane had just landed to refuel on its way back from Bangkok. Would I like him to enquire whether we could hitch a lift back to England? We had just forty-five minutes left before the traffic controllers were due to walk out. We took off for Luton in the nick of time, with tremendous gratitude to God for rescuing us in true cavalry style. We had learnt that we should pray first rather than at the last minute. Our practical experience in Romania had helped us to keep a true perspective when we returned to our academic studies at home.

When we arrived in Luton we contacted our coach driver, who was waiting for us at Heathrow, to say that we would get another coach and join him there. He greeted us with some devastating news. A fire had destroyed the college games room where all our aid was stored. The wall heaters had been left on by mistake. The whole building was now just a charred wreck. I felt an overwhelming sense of disbelief that while we were having a great time ministering in Romania, this dreadful situation was developing back home. Throughout the week a number of helpers had tried to clear up the mess and salvage what they could.

Fortunately for the students of Spurgeon's College, the games room was renovated within a couple of months and to a higher standard than before.

But that was not the last of the bad news. Our truck had broken down on the Romanian-Hungarian border and was stuck in Budapest waiting to be repaired. In Romania our drivers had filled it with diesel which, unbeknown to them, was dirty and full of grit. It was uncertain whether the drivers would be home in time for Christmas.

The first day back in Britain was spent talking to the truck hire company, which said that it would sort out the problem as soon as the truck was back in England. I also contacted the local press about the fire, and an appeal was put out, which resulted in a new load of aid arriving in time for our next scheduled truck to leave for Romania. But our drivers were still stuck in Budapest, and some of them were suffering from health problems. In the end they arrived home the day before Christmas Eve.

Some of our team would never be the same again after seeing the needs of the world beyond the shores of Britain. I do believe that experience of world mission is a valuable aspect of theological training. Five years later, two of the students who had accompanied us on the mission joined the Baptist Missionary Society and went, one to Albania, the other to Italy.

Childcare

Throughout 1991, aid continued to flow into Romania. Over a two-year period, aid worth more than £1 million was donated, filling some two hundred trucks, which trundled their way into every corner of the country, where their contents were distributed through the Baptist Church network. But I was conscious that more than the distribution of aid was necessary if the nation was going to get on its feet. As somebody once said, 'By giving a man a fish you feed him for a day, but by teaching a man to fish you feed him for life.'

By the end of 1991 I had finished my studies and taken up a post as Director of Communications for Spurgeon's College. My work brought me into contact with Spurgeon's Child Care, and I suggested to its directors that it involve Romania in its concerns.

They agreed, and we planned a five-day exploratory visit to Romania to take place in December.

We were again met by Dr Vasile Talpos of the Baptist seminary in Bucharest, who showed us how the seminary had grown since I was last there. More students were attending and more courses were being provided. The equipment we had delivered the previous year was being put to good use. We also witnessed the delivery of a million Bibles from the British and Foreign Bible Society, as well as further aid for students and needy pastors. East European Ministries, which had been established as the umbrella organization to oversee our work in Romania, had been sponsoring a number of pastors for a three-year study period and supplying funds to help establish new churches.

The next day we flew to Iasi in a decrepit, well-worn propeller-driven plane with bucket seats on the floor. We felt like parachutists in an RAF Hercules. We were somewhat disconcerted to find that we had to sit with bags of mail on our laps, the flight being part of the Romanian mail service.

When we landed in Iasi, we were alarmed to see tanks and gun turrets at the airport, which was occupied by soldiers. Threatening noises from neighbouring Moldavia had led to a rise in tension over illegal immigrants. The Moldavians feared a takeover by the aggressive Romanian authorities and were nervously guarding their border.

In Iasi we met John and Rebecca Gacea, with whom I had stayed eighteen months before. Trained veterinarians, they had been unable to find sufficient work, and were left to oversee their church when its pastor suddenly resigned and allegedly emigrated to America after amassing sufficient dollars. This was not an uncommon experience for a church. Pastors and their families were not immune to the lure of a better lifestyle in the West.

John showed us around the church and a church plant which I had seen on my last visit. Both had grown substantially and a second plant was now being established, as well as children's work, which particularly interested my fellow travellers, David Culwick and Alex Morton, Directors of Spurgeon's Child Care. A kindergarten was running, but there was a great lack of qualified staff, finance and resources, elements which Spurgeon's could help with. I had chosen to take David and Alex to eastern

Romania because so far most aid had gone to the main towns in the west of the country, such as Oradea, Arad and Timisoara. Very few trucks had travelled across Romania and over the mountain range to the borders of Moldavia.

We then visited Pastor Dinu Pop, who pastored several churches in Vaslui, where we again saw a kindergarten project and met local Christians. The conditions in which our hosts lived were so basic as to be unbelievable. There was a single hotplate on which all the food was cooked, and a big brick chimney in the centre of the main lounge was all that heated the entire house. As guests, we three were given the lounge floor to sleep on, and even though it was −15°C outside, because the fire had been stoked up for our comfort it was initially very hot. But by four in the morning, it was extremely chilly.

The next morning we heard activity around us as Dinu stoked up the boiler in the bathroom to provide hot water so that we could wash before breakfast. To do this, however, we had to leave the house and pick our way across the courtyard between the chickens, cats, dogs, ducks and pigs, to reach the outhouse where we could make ourselves clean.

Care for the whole community

During that day, we visited a number of orphanages in the area. One in particular had received a lot of aid from Germany and Sweden, and was complete with deep-freezes, refrigerators, big domestic cooking units, food, clothes and medicines. It had a high wall around it, topped with barbed wire, and alarmed in a manner reminiscent of Fort Knox. Again, this was not to keep the children in the orphanage, but to keep out thieves. Sadly, there was bitterness towards the orphanage children for receiving much of the aid that was coming from the West while others remained in poverty. This had developed to such an extent that a number of convoys had been hijacked at gunpoint and relieved of their contents. Any long-term project established in Romania must be of benefit to the whole community. My colleagues from Spurgeon's Child Care were hoping to establish daycare for children by setting up kindergartens and pre-school centres.

Later, we visited the main civic centre, where one of the local churches met for worship on a Sunday. Here, with great pride, the church's members showed us a Christian library consisting of about fifty books, which would have been banned if Ceaucescu were still in power. We also visited a local market, a hive of activity where local people sold everything from cockerels to herbs, and where we could see a number of western products for sale that may well have been taken from well-meaning convoys.

We spotted a number of people, Moldavians, who had crossed the border a few miles away. They were standing barefoot on this freezing December day, selling their shoes to raise money for their families. It was the most pitiful sight I had seen in a long time. Moldavians were far poorer even than Romanians, and had received very little attention from the West.

We walked around Vaslui, looking at a number of other orphanages and hospitals, before returning to Iasi to catch our plane to Bucharest, only to find that it had been cancelled for lack of fuel. We caught the train instead, which, in contrast to the last train I had caught in Romania, was warm and well-lit.

Within five years, Spurgeon's Child Care had opened eight family centres as a result of that visit, providing facilities for over five hundred children and employment for forty staff. Creches, preschool activities, kindergartens, after-school care, food and clothing stations, counselling, holiday camps and literacy programmes are all on offer. It is remarkable how God has blessed this work.

East European Ministries also provided Dr Talpos at the seminary with a car, food, books and help with healthcare. Church twinning, partnership projects and aid for pastors rank among the developments that have taken place. A number of Romanian students have come to England to study theology. The long-term growth of Romania continues, and, although the initial interest from many has dwindled, it is good to see a firm commitment to the country from some organizations.

In particular, the London Baptist Association, which represents approximately three hundred Baptist churches and thirty thousand members in the capital, has established a strong link with Baptists in Bucharest. At the London Baptist Association Autumn Assembly in October 1997, Dr Talpos spoke of his gratitude for the support, encouragement and help given by

London Baptists over the past seven years. 'The greatest need today', he said, 'is for theologically trained pastors and church leaders. They need to be equipped to handle God's Word, so that the amazing growth and church-planting that have taken place throughout Eastern Europe may by sustained in the decades and centuries that lie ahead. Creative Christian social, medical, educational, employment and childcare enterprises are to be encouraged, as churches and people alike equip themselves for the future. Romania, along with most of the other East European countries, battles amid turbulent days of transition, and faces excessively high inflation, unemployment, and political changes resulting from the seventy-year-long Communist era. It is important to remember that over two thirds of European Baptists are to be found in Eastern Europe, and our brothers and sisters in the East still desperately need our encouragement as they seek to proclaim the good news of Jesus Christ to their compatriots.'

Some facts and figures: Romania today

Population

Total 23,816,000

Romanians	81%
Hungarians	7.9%
Gypsies	9%
Germans	0.6%
Turks	150,000
Serbs	80,000
Ukrainians	67,000
Slovaks	34,000
Jews	21,500

Population of Bucharest 2,231,000

	Congregations	Members	Affiliated
Reformed Hussite	1,786	500,000	715,000
Baptist Union	1,300	230,000	330,000
Pentecostal	1,740	208,000	320,000
Brethren	571	80,000	160,000
Seventh Day Adventists	521	65,000	130,000
Augsburg Confession	141	73,500	105,000
Hungarian Baptist	200	20,000	33,300
Lutheran	30	15,000	32,000
Roman Catholic	1,151	756,000	1,050,000
Greek Catholic	140	100,000	600,000
Romanian Orthodox	12,347	11,900,000	17,000,000
Lord's Army		300,000	750,000
Armenian Apostolic	19	8,400	12,000
Jehovah's Witnesses	226	19,030	29,300
All others	186	15,675	24,590

Missionaries to Romania: 165, associated with 38 agencies, *i.e.* 1 for every 141,000 people.

6

BULGARIA AND MACEDONIA, 1992
Filling the vacuum

Before the fall of Communism, Bulgaria was referred to as the 'sixteenth republic of the USSR' (which was made up of fifteen republics) because it followed Soviet policy so closely. Bulgaria has been ruled by many foreign powers in its history, but it did enjoy a period of independence beginning in 1878. The church was not strong enough to provide real opposition when the Communists took over in the mid-1940s. One tenth of the population, the Turks and the Pomarks (people of both Turkish and Bulgarian extraction), were Muslims, and there were many minority groups such as Armenians, Jews, Catholics, Greeks and Protestants. Despite Bulgaria's alliance with Hitler, the Jewish community grew during the Second World War under the courageous protection of King Boris and the national Orthodox Church.

When the Communists came to power, they followed the Soviet anti-religion policy fiercely and tried to assimilate these varied religious communities by force, despite a storm of protest from other governments. The Turks were forced to change their names, and Islamic traditional dress and customs were banned. In May 1989, sixty ethnic Turks were killed in demonstrations against assimilation, and this was followed by expulsion and a huge exodus of Turks across the Turkish border.

Opposition to the government grew in 1989, and many pro-democracy demonstrations took place throughout the country. On 24 October the Communist leadership was thrown into crisis when the foreign minister, Mladenov, resigned after accusing the leader, Todor Zhivkov, of building a personal dictatorship in line with that of Ceaucescu in Romania and Enver Hoxha in Albania. Mladenov moved swiftly to oust Zhivkov by travelling to Moscow to engage Gorbachev's support. On 11 December, the Communist Party announced that a multi-party system would replace the present monopoly, and elections were planned for the spring of 1990. General Zhivkov was put on trial in 1991, accused of embezzlement, and was subsequently imprisoned.

1992: the road to Varna

My first visit to Bulgaria took place in the July of 1992. I had heard much about the country from a Bulgarian student at Spurgeon's College, Evgeniy Naydenov, who came from the Black Sea town of Varna. At home, Evgeniy had been involved in preaching in local churches, along with his father, a lay pastor, and his grandfather, a Baptist minister. He had been recommended by the Bulgarian Baptist Union and awarded a bursary from the Overseas Scholarship Fund to undertake a degree at Spurgeon's. Evgeniy told us how his grandfather had spent six years in prison for preaching the gospel in Bulgaria under the harsh Communist regime of the 1950s and 60s.

With the fall of Communism in Bulgaria, the door was open to accept an invitation from the Baptist Union in that country. With a team of students and friends I flew out to Sofia to meet Evgeniy and the President of the Baptist Union, Rev. Dr Theodore Anglov, and to share in a week of ministry to local churches. Five different cities were covered by our team, while I spent the week visiting churches throughout the country.

With Evgeniy and his parents I drove the three hundred miles from the capital to Varna. My first impression of Bulgaria was of a country not as undeveloped as Romania, but not quite as advanced as Hungary or Poland. We drove out of the great city on concrete dual carriageways along the flat plains of central Bulgaria towards the beautiful city of Plovdiv. There we met with some of Evgeniy's relatives and saw the local Baptist church, which, since the fall of Communism, had grown from just a handful of faithful Christians to a vibrant fellowship bursting at the seams, with two hundred members. They were worshipping in a converted house, with a lounge and other rooms downstairs, and the upstairs bedrooms in use as Sunday-school rooms. The building was in a rather precarious state, having suffered somewhat during an earthquake some years before. The church's members wanted to build a new church into which they could expand further, a desire shared by many churches and Christian organizations all over Eastern Europe.

As sunset approached, we made our way from Plovdiv to Kazanlak at the base of the mountain range we needed to cross to reach Varna. We stopped and explored its fascinating cobbled streets, rich in history. Kazanlak was the first small village to have an established Baptist church, and also the first place to witness baptisms, at the end of the 1800s. Two preachers, Gregor Dumnikoff and Petro Kirkilanoff, bought a copy of the gospels, and were joined by others as they discovered for themselves, without outside help, the truth contained there. They advertised in the newspapers of Sofia and Rustchuk for someone to come and baptize them. As a result two German Baptist preachers, Kargel and Palamedoff, arrived to perform the baptisms, and a Russian Baptist, Vasili Tartargeoff, became their pastor and discipled them in the faith.

The Baptists to whom the Kazanlak believers appealed had diverse origins. As early as 1867 the British and Foreign Bible Society employed two Polish pastors as colporteurs for northeastern Bulgaria. In 1869 J. G. Oncken encouraged the work of Martin Heringer and evangelist Jakob Klundt, two men who were vital to the growth of the Baptist Church in Bulgaria. Later pastors and evangelists were also ethnic Bulgarians, Russians or Germans.

Our car wove its way up hairpin bends to the top of a mountain, and we looked back over the plains at a magnificent sunset, which illuminated the gold dome of Kazanlak's Orthodox church, before we completed the last hour and a half of our journey.

The mighty banana

The next day I was free to explore Varna. Its beautiful golden beaches attract holidaymakers from around Bulgaria, Russia, Germany, Romania and even the UK. The high street was an exciting place for me to observe Bulgarian life. As I sat Parisian-style at a pavement table, drinking coffee, I noted the mix of people in the town. There were a considerable number of Bulgarian Gypsies, pure Bulgarians, Turks, Pomarks, Romanian refugees and a few tourists. It was obvious that the young people out and about were enjoying their new-found liberty to the full. The western film *Pretty Woman* had just been released at the local cinema, and all the girls were imitating Julia Roberts by wearing black miniskirts and knee-high boots. Unable to afford cars, people posed by walking up and down the main street with a banana or two. This fruit had been unavailable in Bulgaria for years, but was now imported, and was quite expensive. If you could afford a banana, you were a cool dude. It was a very strange sight to behold.

Varna relies heavily on the tourist industry, having many souvenir shops, cafés, hotels, night clubs and fairground activities, all of which depend on the summer trade to see them through the winter months. The town also has a large port which provides employment for local residents.

The next day I went with Evgeniy to the Varna Baptist Church, where Evgeniy's grandfather still served as a pastor, along with Boggidar Igoff, General Secretary of the Baptist Union of Bulgaria. Boggidar also broadcast a weekly Bible study programme on Transworld Radio. For many of his listeners, the only way to hear the gospel was on the airwaves, as churches did not exist in every town or village. I was delighted to see a large number of young people in the church that Sunday morning. They formed about 60% of the congregation. Forty newcomers were being welcomed as members after their baptisms the previous week. The church had baptized some hundred and fifty new converts in the last two years, a reflection of the increased interest in Christianity throughout Bulgaria as a whole.

Before the fall of Communism, there were about sixteen registered Baptist churches in Bulgaria, containing around six hundred members. Just two years later, there were thirty-six churches with over six thousand members (and by 1997 this had grown to sixty-six churches). In addition to these, twenty-five evangelical churches had been established by one Pastor Mitko of Sandanski, but theological differences had prevented them from joining the Baptist Union. These new churches tended to be more charismatic than Union members. Their livelier worship attracted young people. Throughout Eastern Europe, Pentecostal or house churches have flourished alongside the more traditional churches, an interesting development noted also in the West.

After the service, Evgeniy's grandfather spoke to me about the cost of refusing to deny one's faith in Communist Bulgaria. He told of how, on some days, food in the prison consisted of very watery soup and mouldy stale bread, and how some prisoners died in the winter-time because of the lack of heating, warm clothes and medication. Between 1948 and 1952, hundreds of believers were sent to prison and subjected to terrible treatment. A general amnesty was declared in 1964, but most survivors were too traumatized to speak of their experiences. Intense anti-religious education in schools, and discrimination against believers in professional roles, dissuaded people from attending church. An efficient system of police surveillance and intimidation backed by ubiquitous informers within congregations made most Christians unwilling to talk to westerners or to accept gifts of literature or money. As recently as 1982, some Bibles donated by western missionaries were turned over to the police by Christians who feared reprisals. Any visitors to Bulgaria usually followed well-established tourist routes and were unable to attend religious services. Believers here still suffer from a religious seclusion more complete than anywhere else in Eastern Europe, bar Albania. Lack of contact with the rest of the Christian world has sapped Bulgarian Christian life for centuries.

Padlocked for forty years

The next day, Monday, we drove the hundred miles north to Ruse, a town on the Romanian border, where we met with the local Baptist leaders. One of these men, now in his sixties and also called Evgeniy, was a young man of twenty-five when the Communists came to power forty years previously. He told us how they had thrown him out of the church, padlocked the door, and warned that the building would never be used as a place of worship again. The pews were ripped out, the baptistry filled with rubble and concreted over, and the building turned into a social club with a bar and cinema. For forty years, Evgeniy senior, and other faithful members of the church, met in homes. They prayed that one day they would be able to have their place of worship back, and gather again in their house of God, using it for its original purpose. With great emotion, Evgeniy shared with us the moment he had witnessed just months ago, when the authorities came, took the padlock off the church doors and told church members that they could have their building back. Their dedicated prayers had been answered. They had waited forty years, but God had remained faithful and honoured their persistence. The church's members were now busy opening up the baptistry, replastering the walls and putting new window frames in. New pews had been made, and the Christians were hoping to have the church open for services very shortly. They were also building a block of flats at the back of the church to house, among others, a pastor. They were still in need of a pastor, but, though their resources were limited, they were waiting for God to supply one for them.

While in Ruse, I heard the story of how the church was founded. At the end of the last century, a Russian Christian was waiting in Ruse to cross the Danube and leave the country by boat. The river had completely frozen under the harsh winter conditions, and he was stranded in Bulgaria. He spent three weeks in Ruse, using his time to evangelize, preaching in the evenings and leading services in the daytime. By the time he left, a church had been established.

Later that afternoon, Evgeniy junior and I went to visit a local Methodist minister. It was good to hear how the Methodists and Baptists in Ruse were united in their Christian witness.

'Come over to Macedonia'

We returned to Varna from Ruse late in the evening, and had just settled down to relax when the telephone rang. It was a friend of Evgeniy's calling from a church in Skopje, Macedonia.

A few moments later, Evgeniy popped his head around the door and asked, 'Would you like to go to Macedonia tomorrow?'

I replied casually, 'Yes, if you like, that would be great.' If Macedonian Christians wanted us to see something of their situation and form links with them, then we would go. It was only after Evgeniy came off the telephone that I realized how far away it was. Evgeniy said that we would need to leave at 5.00am in order to cover the four hundred miles to Skopje. We filled up the car with petrol plus two full jerrycans, as petrol was rationed in the former Yugoslavia while the conflict raged between Serbs and Croats.

After a short night's sleep we saw a lovely sunrise over the Black Sea coast as we blazed a trail across Bulgaria from east to west, and on to Macedonia. We stopped briefly at Burgas, a holiday town and historic port complete with ancient buildings and cobblestones, a delightful contrast to the high-rise blocks and commercialized, though golden, sands of Varna. We then drove inland across a large plain, and were halted in our tracks as we came across the Bulgarian army on shooting practice. Tanks and artillery were firing from the plains, trying to destroy a barn on the opposite hillside. Shells flew above the road as we tried to drive along it. All that was stopping us was a man with a red flag. We waited in a queue of about twenty cars for forty minutes until we could continue, which we did with understandable trepidation.

After that somewhat nerve-wracking experience, we made good speed across the fertile plain of central Bulgaria, with its massive fruit farms and rows upon rows of shops selling peaches, plums, apples and lemons. We lunched with Evgeniy's relatives in Plovdiv and met briefly with a Christian businessman, who wanted to establish a mineral-water plant in the mountains, but needed US $50,000 to set it up.

As we meandered from the plains up through the southern mountain range of Bulgaria, minarets standing tall in town centres identified this as a Muslim area. This region was also noted for its excellent skiing in winter, but at that moment the trees were in full leaf. It was a beautiful sight.

We reached the border at teatime and left Bulgaria without any trouble. We wondered whether we would be allowed into southern Yugoslavia, since the UN had imposed strict controls.

But the border was busy with trucks *en route* to Serbia via a 'back door'. Soldiers and customs officials knew that fuel and other goods would find their way into Macedonia and be sold on the black market at four times their value. To sell a tank full of fuel would bring rich reward to the courier, who made as much as an average week's wages with each trip.

Molotov cocktail in Skopje

We descended the mountain border on a narrow winding road with a two-hundred-foot drop into a turquoise lake on the left. When we arrived in Skopje, fifteen hours after leaving Varna, we were greeted by the local Baptist pastor, who told us how his modern church had recently celebrated ten baptisms in an open-air homemade concrete baptistry built into the corner of the church. We saw the church's Christian bookshop, a small brick building also in the courtyard, housing just two rows of books, of which the church's members were extremely proud. To a western eye, this was a pitiful sight, but to these Macedonian believers it was a great symbol of freedom and victory after decades of persecution and hardship. The church had three storeys, which included storerooms for aid, living accommodation and church rooms, and rooms for the youth groups and Bible study meetings. It had been built three years ago with money from Germany and the USA.

We spent the night at the home of the pastor's parents, where the congregation had met until the new church was built. We heard stories late into the night of how his father had served the gospel in a little village sixty miles away, where for fifty years he had suffered for his faith. He recounted how on one occasion he had felt the Lord impress upon him the need to hold an open-air service beneath the mountain trees. That Sunday, a Molotov cocktail was thrown through the church window and the building was completely destroyed. The church's members would have been killed had they been meeting there as usual.

Skopje had one of Macedonia's two Baptist churches, and thirty of its fifty Baptists. The other Baptist church and its twenty members were in the pastor's father's village. There were no qualified pastors, yet the church was dedicated to sharing the gospel and helping the many refugees fleeing from Serbia, Croatia and Bosnia. The pastor, a married man of thirty-five with two young children, had studied in the USA. He shared with us his fear that the Serbs would turn south and take control of Macedonia, as they had done in neighbouring Kosova. Another concern was the growth of cults in Macedonia, a concern shared by churches all over Eastern Europe. The fall of Communism left a great spiritual vacuum which many religious groups were trying to fill.

The next morning we left early to return to Sofia. Our flying visit had indeed been brief, but links had been established and would be built on by Christians in both Bulgaria and the UK.

This time we did have problems crossing the border. Because I had left Bulgaria, my visa had been cancelled and we had to wait for a new one to be processed, for which I paid US $50.

We spent the day after that at the beautiful mountain monastery of Rila and the Stob Orphanage, which was being sponsored by members of my home church, among others. The children, many of whom were unfortunately mentally and physically disabled, were enjoying a summer holiday in wood cabins by a mountain river. The air was pure, the river fast-flowing and fresh, and the children were having a wonderful time. New windows and bathrooms were being installed in the orphanage in time for the harsh winter months ahead.

From there we headed to the capital, Sofia, the next day, where we visited the Logos Bible Institute. The institute had three hundred students training part-time, and was building a seminary with funds from the USA, Britain and Germany. We later met up with the rest of my party from the UK, all of whom had wonderful stories to tell about their visit.

On returning home, we found that there was quite an interest in Bulgaria from a number of churches and individuals. After a conversation with representatives of the Evangelical Alliance, a special Bulgarian Day was held in October 1994, attended by Theodore Anglov. As a result of this meeting, the Evangelical Alliance Bulgarian Support Group was established. It now meets four times a year and is actively involved in encouraging the church in Bulgaria through distributing aid, sponsoring pastors and students, planting churches, providing theological works and twinning Bulgarian churches with churches in Britain.

Three years later, in October 1997, a second Bulgarian Consultation Day was held, at which the guest speaker was again Theodore Anglov, who shared how the many students trained in western theological colleges were now teaching in the theological seminaries of Bulgaria, and thus equipping and strengthening pastors and leaders for the future. Much development has taken place with the modernizing and establishing of new churches, yet it was evident that there was still strong opposition from the Orthodox Church, and great hardship with inflation running at 1,000%. It was also recorded that in Macedonia a new religious law had been introduced in 1997, which was restricting evangelism greatly.

For some facts and figures, see pp. 140–141.

7

ALBANIA
The land of the eagle

Albania is a small and remote country lying on the east side of the Adriatic, opposite the boot of Italy and in the southeast of Europe. Formerly a territory of the Ottoman Empire, it declared its independence in November 1912. In November 1944, under the leadership of Enver Hoxha, the Communist-led National Liberation Front took power. In January 1946 Albania was proclaimed a people's republic, of which a sworn constitution was promulgated in March 1946. In December 1981 Albania had a population of 2,752,300, and the capital, Tirana, had 220,000 inhabitants. At the end of the Second World War, over 70% of the population was Muslim, but in 1967 Albania was officially proclaimed the first atheistic state in the world.

Notable religious figures in the twentieth century who were of Albanian origin were the late Ecumenical Patriarch of Constantinople, Athenagoras (who reopened Orthodox discussions with Pope Paul in 1967), and the late Mother Theresa of Calcutta, born of Albanian parents in Skopje, Macedonia, a province of Yugoslavia.

The country is rich in mineral resources: in particular, chromium, copper, iron ore and nickel. It also produces bitumen and coal, and has substantial hydro-electric generating capacity. Agriculture has been completely collectivized. Approximately two-thirds of the population live on the land producing wheat, cotton, tobacco and sugar beet. Albania's most important trade links are with Yugoslavia, Italy, Turkey and Greece.

In 1961 Albania broke off relationships with the Soviet Union and forged links with the People's Republic of China. In 1968 it formally withdrew from the Warsaw Pact and, in fact, Chinese vehicles, trucks and machinery can still be seen throughout Albania today.

In 1984, Amnesty International was extremely concerned about Albania in five particular areas: the imprisonment of prisoners of conscience; legislation severely restricting the exercise of internationally recognized human rights; breaches of internationally recognized standards of fair trial; allegations of torture and ill-treatment of detainees, especially during investigating procedures; and the use of the death penalty.

The Albanian constitution embodies the principles formulated by Marx, Engels, Lenin and Stalin, especially in the field of the theory of dictatorship. The proletariat population was fed daily through the *Voice of the People* (*Zei I Pullit*), the Communist daily newspaper which contained lies and untruths about the West.

In practice, it appeared that people who expressed views critical of the economic or political conditions in the country were liable to be persecuted, even if their criticisms were voiced in private conversations. A number of former political prisoners told Amnesty International that they were convicted on the basis of the testimony of informers or plain-clothes Sigurumi officials who, in some cases, had deliberately provoked them to criticize the authorities. One former prisoner said he was jailed for three years and interned for another three because of conversations with acquaintances, in which he had spoken of the 1973 and 1978 revolts in the Spac labour camp. He alleged that two Sigurumi agents present during the conversation had reported him to the authorities.

(Source: *Albania – Political Imprisonment and the Law*, Amnesty International, 1984)

According to the Keston Institute, in late 1988, a group of Dutch tourists visiting Albania provoked an incident when they began to give out copies of the New Testament to factory workers. The authorities sealed off the factory, confiscated all copies of the New Testament and then burned them in the factory yard. The tourists, members of an independent Protestant church, were given a stern warning by the authorities. Their bus was searched thoroughly, and a further hundred Bibles were discovered and confiscated.

In November 1986, Dr and Mrs Edwin Jacques, evangelical missionaries who served in the American mission school in Korce from 1932 to 1940, were granted visas for a ten-day visit after having been refused periodically for forty years.

Between July and September 1988, three Albanian clergymen from abroad visited Albania for a brief period. The Rev. Arthur E. Liolin, the American-born Chancellor of the Albanian Orthodox Diocese in America, toured Albania for approximately three weeks in July and August. He was apparently the first clergyman since 1967 to visit and travel round the country wearing clerical garb.

The Rev. Iman Ishmael, Director of the Albanian Islamic Centre of Detroit, an Albanian-born American citizen, was permitted to visit Albania with his family for twenty days in August. He had been applying every year since 1962 for a visa to visit his native land.
(Source: *Albania: Religion in a Fortress State*, April 1989)

'Tomorrow you die'

In the spring of 1978, I was on a radio course with the Worldwide Evangelization Crusade (now WEC International), and met a thirty-year old man from Albania called Sali Rachmani. As we got to know each other, I was shocked to learn first-hand that Albanian Christians were not allowed to own or read Bibles or to worship freely, and that they were persecuted. Sali was a very bubbly man with a round, happy, smiling face, who spoke with passion and the swiftness of an automatic machine gun as he asked and answered questions. He told me how faithful Christian believers in Albania had been killed, and others imprisoned, because they would not renounce their faith in Jesus Christ. Still others were beaten and flogged.

After the course, Sali and I kept in touch and I developed a desire to visit his far-off atheistic country. Over the next fourteen years I gleaned every piece of information about Albania that I could from the news and Christian books, and prayed fervently for this nation and the Christians there. I devoured a book by Reona Peterson, called *Tomorrow You Die* (YWAM), telling of how she ventured into Albania as a tourist. Reona smuggled in gospel tracts and gave them to hotel staff and any Albanians that she met. She was arrested, put in a prison cell and told fiercely by guards, 'Tomorrow you die.' Eventually she was expelled from the country and told never to come back.

But Reona did go back. For forty years, Albania was the least evangelized country in Europe. But when the new day of freedom dawned, hundreds of young people went to Albania under the banner of Youth With A Mission and at Reona's instigation. In the summer of 1992, teams from YWAM visited Albania to distribute fifty thousand tracts to homes in Tirana. Since then, further teams have been working in villages, not only promoting the gospel, but also helping with aid, literacy classes and health programmes as they seek to share the unconditional love of Christ.

For many years Albania was Europe's most closed country, but in May 1990, as part of the domino effect of the fall of other Eastern European Communist states, it underwent a pro-democracy revolution and religion was once again made a matter of personal choice.

History and religion

Albania has a history of occupation. From about the fifteenth century to the twentieth, Albanians failed to resist the occupation of the Turks, and did not finally free themselves from Turkey until 1912.

Albanians are largely descendants of the Illyrians, who occupied most of the Balkans before the Slavs. In the time of the Roman Empire, Illyricum was possibly better governed, more prosperous and more integrated into European culture than the area has been at any time since. The Slav occupation of AD 60 to 800 destroyed much of Roman civilization, but Christianity survived. The bishopric of Durres had been established in AD 66, its bishop, Astio, being one of the earliest Christian martyrs. By the eleventh century, however, the church had split. Soon Albania came under the sway of the Orthodox Patriarch of Constantinople, while the north stood with Rome, though few Albanians were aware of the doctrinal differences.

In 1385, the Turks invaded. Despite fierce resistance under a leader known as Skanderberg, from 1405 to 1468 Albania was engulfed by the Islamic Ottoman Empire. Conversion to Islam was slow, and at first involved only feudal landowners eager to retain their property and status.

In the fifteenth century the Catholic Church was still active and well organized. In 1616, the Bishop of Bar was able to report that only 10% of Albanians had converted to Islam. By the end of the seventeenth century, however, with a decline in pastoral standards, higher taxes on Christians and increased coercion, there were more conversions to the Muslim faith. Under such conditions it was hardly surprising that among Albanians, who are not naturally a religious people, Islam rarely went very deep. Some joined the Bektashi (more popularly known as the Dervishes), a pantheistic, charismatic, tolerant, and heretical Muslim sect. Bektashi mixed pagan, Christian and Muslim elements. Albanians found them congenial; the Albanian version is a compound of popular mysticism and Masonic-style cult, majoring on secret signs. There are also many pagan customs over in Kosova, where resident Albanians were not pressurized to conform to Communism; children were still occasional victims of blood feud.

When Albania gained independence, it remained under the supervision of the great powers. In 1913, nearly half of the lands where Albanians were settled were allotted by the London Conference to the Montenegrins and the Serbs. Some became part of Yugoslavia. Albania also continued to suffer from misrule during the reign of King Zog, a clan chief who seized power in 1924. He became a puppet of Mussolini's Italy, which was allowed to exploit the country as a colony. Zog fled to Britain and used gold looted from the Albanian treasury to rent a floor at London's Ritz Hotel.

When Italy invaded in 1939, over 80% of the country was illiterate, and the country had no university. Health problems abounded, half the babies born died in their early months of life, and government corruption was notorious, even by Balkan standards. Albania was primitive.

In 1939, the Catholic church had 124,000 members in 123 parishes, served by 152 priests, thirty-two lay monks and 135 nuns. They operated a seminary, fifteen schools, 134 orphanages and a lively press. Franciscans and Jesuits made heroic attempts to reconcile and pacify warring clans in the mountains. Living in remote villages, they acted as judges and as doctors, trudging from deathbed to deathbed during epidemics, and were greatly beloved. Nuns helped to pioneer the education of girls and staff the few hospitals.

On 8 November 1941 the Albanian Communist Party was founded, with Enver Hoxha playing a leading role until his death in April 1985. Albanians were trained to hate foreigners and to use guns, traditionally the Albanian's best friend.

In 1977, Fr Fran Mark Gjoni was sentenced to twelve years in a labour camp when Bibles and other religious literature were discovered in his attic. Under torture he admitted that he had found them in parks and on the sea shore, and was storing them in anticipation of the day when religion would once again be legal. Although not reported by the press, the trial aroused much interest among Albanians, many of whom were aware that certain Christian groups of the West floated literature in plastic bags that washed up on the Albanian coast. It is estimated that between 1979 and 1982, western Christians somehow managed to smuggle in 30,000 gospels. Secret messages were smuggled out of Albania to western Christians, declaring that 'the church of Jesus Christ is alive and growing in Albania; please send us more literature'.

The fall of Stalinism

Enver Hoxha was born in Gjirokaster in Albania, where his father was a Muslim draper. He was an oppressive atheist of the most thoroughgoing Stalinist persuasion, and an extreme patriot. He took advantage of American and French schooling and a university career in Montpelier and Brussels, and in the Second World War he took his chance to rise to be head of the Albania Communist Workers' Party. He became Prime Minister in 1944, and from 1954 took up the post of first Secretary of the party. Khruschev's fall drove him into the arms of the more extreme Chinese Communists, and, though he secured economic aid from them, even they proved too lax for him. He made atheism a state imperative and turned his back on the civilized world. His personal brutality left its mark on the memory of those who knew him and yet survived.

In 1978, Albania broke with China and for many years exercised a policy of isolationism. The regime was one of ruthless internal control based on orthodox Stalinism and nationalism. The ratio of secret police per head of the population was the highest in Europe, and, while the privileges granted to Communist officials were widely resented, few dared to show any outward disapproval. Enver Hoxha built up a personal cult which, after his death, was taken over by his protégé and successor, Ramiz Alia.

Throughout 1989 the country seemed relatively untouched by the pro-democracy revolution which was sweeping throughout the rest of Communist Eastern Europe. In January 1990, however, reports began to reach the West of large anti-government demonstrations in Albania. A Yugoslav news agency reported that crowds had tried to pull down a large statue of Stalin, but had been restrained by the police using tear gas and truncheons. Later in 1990, President Alia responded to growing unrest by declaring reforms of the notorious penal code. Freedom of speech and of religion were granted for the first time under the Communist government, and emigration was also allowed.

A huge wave of Albanians fled continuing upheaval and poverty for a new life in the West. In July 1990, more than five thousand Albanians stormed embassies in Tirana, climbing walls and demanding permission to emigrate. The government was forced to let them leave the country, in what became known as 'the great escape'. Since then, the exodus of refugees has continued, although high walls have been constructed around all western embassies. An entire Jewish community was allowed to leave, as well as thousands of Albanians of Greek origin.

Anti-government demonstrations continued until December, when the first reports of troops firing on demonstrators reached the West. Stalin's statue in Tirana's main square was quietly removed by the authorities one night at midnight. Elections were held and the ruling Democratic Forum Party was opposed by a number of others, including the non-Communist Democratic Party. Although the government was re-elected, mainly by a largely rural population who feared change, it failed to survive, and in June 1991 a government of national unity was formed to rule until another round of elections could be held.

In the weeks running up to the elections, riots between demonstrators and police were commonplace, and students went on hunger strike to demand that Enver Hoxha's name be removed from the university. The big statue of Hoxha was toppled by ecstatic crowds as riot police tried in vain to control the demonstrators. News reports in the West depicted amazing scenes reminiscent of Dunkirk, as crowds of Albanians clung to overcrowded departing ships. Mediterranean ports could no longer cope with the influx of boats, of all shapes and sizes, which were crossing the Adriatic for Corfu, Greece and Italy. After several days of international embarrassment for Italy, many of the refugees, who had only a minimal amount of food and water, were sent back to Albania. Many were glad to return home. Italy, alarmed by a continuing flood of economic refugees, decided to send several hundred troops to Albania to organize the distribution of humanitarian aid as the autumn of 1991 began. Appeals for direct aid were made throughout the rest of Europe.

'The religion of Albania is Albanianism'

According to official statistics, three-quarters of Albanians are now atheists, 20% are Muslims and 5% are Christians. About half of these are Orthodox, found largely in the south, and half Catholic, in the north. Under Communist rule, religious activity of any kind could result in imprisonment, but services and baptisms were conducted secretly, out of view of the authorities.

Christianity came to Albania early on in the country's history, probably brought by Greek traders. When the whole area was occupied by the Turks, the Christian population was taxed and many converted to Islam. By 1912, Albania had become the only country in Europe with a Muslim majority, though, under Hoxha, all religions were persecuted and religion was considered a superstition and divisive force. The Communists had a slogan: 'The religion of Albania is Albanianism.'

In 1967 Hoxha launched a campaign to close down all places of worship. The constitution of 1976 declared that the state recognized no religion, and instead supported the advancement of atheistic propaganda to promote a materialist worldview among the people.

By May 1967, all of Albania's 2,169 places of worship, including about six hundred Orthodox and 327 Catholic churches, had been vandalized, closed or converted to what the state termed 'more useful' secular purposes, such as cafés, sports stadiums, barns, secret-police headquarters, public toilets, games halls or workers' apartments. Clergy were publicly ridiculed and beaten. A Franciscan church and a friary in Shkroder were burnt to the ground at night, and four elderly Franciscans sleeping inside were burnt to death. According to the party daily, *Zei I Pollit*, 217 clergy were sentenced to prison or labour camps for re-education, and five thousand Christians were sent on a six-month brainwashing course. One bishop, Ernest Koba, was beaten unconscious when he refused to recant his faith. He was later seen wheeling a dustcart. Other clergy were forced to do manual labour. Elderly clergy were ordered to return to their birthplace and were refused ration cards.

According to Amnesty International, a group of Orthodox priests were defrocked publicly and their beards forcibly shaved off as a crowd jeered. The one priest who resisted was reported to have been sentenced to eight years' imprisonment for anti-state agitation. Many Catholic priests and monks were given long jail sentences. Fr Gege Lumaj was sentenced in 1967 to seven years' imprisonment which was later increased to a total of twenty-two years. Fr Mark Hasi was given a twenty-year sentence and Fr Zef Pllumbi fifteen years. Other priests, such as Fr Kiri, Fr Harapi and Fr Benedict Dema, suffered severe deprivation or died of starvation because the ration cards necessary to buy food and clothing were taken away from them.

One priest, Fr Marin Shkurti, who fled from Albania to Yugoslavia in January 1968, was recaptured and brought back to Albania, where he was bound and dragged behind a truck for twenty-five miles to the city of Shkroder while his family looked on. He was then executed before a crowd of three thousand. His family members received long prison sentences.

'No-one shall be condemned for believing'

Despite the intensity and brutality of such anti-religion campaigns, religion survived in Albania. Many of the older church generation retained their religious practices learnt in the pre-Communist era, and passed them on to a new generation of believers. Even in the absence of clergy, parents secretly carried out the customs and traditions of their faith as taught by their own parents. Fathers would baptize their children with only the mother and perhaps a few trusted relatives present. With churches closed, believers risked a three-year prison sentence to listen to

Christian broadcasts from Vatican Radio, Radio Rome, Radio Florina in Greece, Radio Cairo and evangelical Protestant stations such as Radio Monte Carlo. These weekly broadcasts were a spiritual lifeline to many Albanian believers.

One letter recorded in the Keston News Service in January 1991 read as follows:

Our churches were destroyed, our hearts mournful, but the faithful gathered secretly in the dark of the night near church ruins and inasmuch as we had icons we beheld the dome of the heavens which the Lord himself created with his own hand, star after star after star. This gave us courage to wait until the Lord would rebuild our churches for worship, churches which had been turned into stables for animals and ruinous dwellings. You could never imagine our sufferings during the past forty-five years, ever! A people with a deep-rooted culture will never permit its faith to be eliminated. In Albania, the cultured youth would not allow the cross in their hearts to be removed. From university students to villagers; even Muslims helped us as they knew that their parents or grandparents were once Christians. Our group baptized in secret, babies, adults and even Muslims. Jesus had given us heart and quietly we did the Lord's work for our Saviour Jesus Christ. Then what freedom came! The law was removed – 'No-one shall be condemned for believing.' We went to former church sites in our tens of thousands all over Albania, witnessing to the world that we are not 'an atheistic people'.

This letter confirms what was suspected but not known by observers in the West. Religious belief had continued in atheistic Albania throughout the years that it had been illegal.

In May 1990, the law banning religious propaganda was lifted and shortly afterwards churches and mosques were allowed to reopen. President Alia said that since everyone had the right to be an atheist, they should also have the right to believe. The Albanian leadership had for many years maintained that no religious activity took place in the land, and that there were no religious prisoners. These claims were proved false. In April 1989 Fr Simon Jubani, a Catholic priest, was released after twenty-six years in prison. Another priest was released after twenty years. A further twenty-six Catholic priests were released from custody, while the fate of many other prisoners of conscience is still unknown, though it is likely that they were killed.

The Easter of 1990 was the first that Christians had been allowed to celebrate publicly for over four decades. Fr Jubani led about a thousand people in a Mass in Rmajit. At Christmas it was reliably reported that thousands of people were attending Christmas and Epiphany services. In the summer of 1991 it was possible for foreign Christians to enter Albania, and a hundred missionaries from all over the world joined the first evangelistic campaign in that country for over fifty years. Over eight thousand Albanians came to a stadium in Tirana to hear the Word of God, and at the end of the week more than two hundred came to the first meeting at a new evangelical church.

I tried to get a visa for the event in Tirana after hearing that my friend Sali would be attending, but the lack of an Albanian embassy in Britain hindered my chances. Any attempt could be made only through an embassy in Paris, and I was not successful. My desire to visit this once forbidden and, to me, mystical land persisted.

In the September of 1992, I was at my desk, praying for Albania and pleading with the Lord for an opportunity to go there, when a friend rang to tell me that there was a spare seat in a light aircraft flying to that country in a week's time. I would be accompanying my friend, a dentist, an optician and a news reporter, as well as the member of my friend's church who owned the aircraft.

8

ALBANIA, 1992
Poverty and philosophy

A week later, we were flying over the flat coastline of Albania and into Tirana International Airport, which, despite its grand title, was simply a tower and an airstrip. At first, we were unable to land because a herd of cows was grazing on the runway, while a number of elderly farmers cycled down it and children played hopscotch on it. Once they had all moved out of the way, we landed and were greeted personally by airport officials who asked how long we were planning to stay in Albania. When we told them we were going to stay for eight days, they were amazed that we wanted to be there for so long.

Our pilot, Stan, showed the officials a letter we had from the Minister of Agriculture granting us permission to deliver aid to Albania. We unloaded and made our way through immigration, which gave us no trouble at all, to an arrival lounge with broken tiles on the floor, no glass in the windows and a dingy, barn-like feel. Adults and children were staring at us as if we had just dropped from Mars.

Outside, we were greeted by our Albanian contacts, who met us in a big white Land Rover, which had been donated by Stan's organization, Light to Albania, on his previous visit. As we walked the hundred yards to this vehicle, we were jostled by children. Driving down the bumpy, dusty roads to the city, we noticed stumps indicating that this road had previously been an avenue. The trees had been chopped down for firewood by local people, a crime for which, under Hoxha, they would have been imprisoned.

We made our way through the busy, narrow streets of Tirana, weaving in and around the massive potholes and the hustling and bustling people walking and cycling about their afternoon business. It was fascinating to observe the colourful signs of Albanian life and culture around us. In the months since relative freedom had returned to the land, every house on a main street seemed to have been turned into a kiosk, selling everything from Coca Cola to nappies, cigarettes and CDs.

Redina's story

Our welcoming party included a twenty-year-old Albanian woman called Redina Kolaneci, from Korce, a large town about a hundred miles to the east near the Macedonian border. Redina's father was a professor of mathematics at Tirana University and her mother was an English teacher. Redina herself spoke perfect English. She was a lively, vivacious, round-faced young woman who radiated the joy of the Lord. She had been a Christian for nearly a year, and she shared her remarkable testimony with us as we drove along. I will let Redina tell the story:

Prior to going to the University of Tirana, where I studied philosophy, I met some British tourists in 1986 when I was still at high school. Little did I know then that these tourists who came to our English class were Christians travelling across Albania and praying that God would touch the lives of Albanian people and bring them to a knowledge of himself. I became very friendly with two of the people in the group and I kept in touch with these families for several years. This fact was very amazing, especially considering the censoring of all letters which was very strong in Albania at the time. But none of the letters we exchanged went missing. This was truly a miracle.

So it was, through these two British Christian families, that I first heard about God and was given a copy of the

Scriptures. One of my British friends came back to Albania in 1991 and he told me first about Christ and put me in touch with a group of missionaries.

During the final years of my studies at Tirana University in 1991–2, I wrote my degree thesis on the role of Christian ethics in the life of society. This topic caused quite a stir among the academics, since many of my tutors were firm atheists who did not want to introduce any Christian topics into the university agenda. Because I happened to be a good student, however, they decided that I should work on the topic I had chosen. It was a great privilege for me and my supervisor, Mr John Quanrud, pastor of one of the evangelical churches in Tirana, to present the first modest study as part of an Albanian university degree, which took in consideration the influence of Christian faith on society.

Redina became one of the leaders of the Christian student movement at the University of Tirana, and when freedom came, Redina, who had been a Christian for barely two months, was given regular slots as an agony aunt on radio and television.

Redina took us to her aunt's house, where we were given a meal. While we were eating, we heard the sound of gunfire coming from behind the house. An argument had broken out between two men, and one of them had pulled out a gun and shot the other three times in the head. The precarious state of Albanian politics had given rise to a lawlessness which intruded on everyday life.

Chamber of horrors

The conditions in which Redina's aunt lived were somewhat primitive compared to the standards we were used to. A visit to the bathroom revealed the toilet to be a hole in the ground, and the same room was used as a shower room and for washing clothes. The floors were covered with a threadbare carpet, and carpets were hung on the walls, a common practice in Eastern European countries. The only lighting came from a single 25 watt bulb, which, under Hoxha, was all that had been allowed to each family.

As night began to fall upon Tirana, I discovered that Redina's home town of Korce was our destination, some four hours away over rugged mountain roads. When we arrived at her parents' house it was 1.30am. We were given a meal and taken to our accommodation on the other side of town.

The next day we were given a guided tour of the local hospital, which appeared to be a place more hazardous to health than beneficial. The rooms were dark and dingy, and children slept six to a bed in disgusting sheets. The smell was appalling, and we could see very few doctors and nurses and little medical equipment. Most of the windows were broken and the furniture and floors had all seen better days.

The healthier patients were outside in the courtyard, hoping to gain some strength from the sunshine and fresh air, away from the damp, pungent smell of the stale air in the dark wards. Here an eighteen-year-old Muslim man challenged me about Christianity. He asked me who Jesus was, so I explained the gospel to him. He kept firing questions at me, and a crowd gathered round us. I jumped up on to a low wall and preached for the next forty minutes about all that Christ had achieved on the cross, and how he had purchased salvation for all who would believe in him. This was a wonderful spontaneous opportunity to share the good news of Jesus Christ, which was the purpose of my visit to Albania. I was able to answer some of the tough questions fired at me by these Albanian Muslims, as well as distribute tracts in Albanian which I had been given by the Scripture Gift Mission.

We continued our tour of the hospital in the main operating theatre. Most of its light seemed to come from one 100 watt bulb and an open window which acted as a passage for flies. We walked round the baby wards and the maternity unit, where we saw that some of the children had been born with deformities to mothers who were malnourished and lived harsh lives in the villages.

We then visited the dental unit, which was in no better condition than the hospital; in fact, it looked worse. The ripped, antiquated dental chair looked as though it should have been in a museum, along with the rest of the equipment. The cabinet, housing what medication there was, had broken glass in it. The spitoon was covered in blood, and all over the floor were cotton-wool balls soaked in congealed blood. It was with a sense of irony that we noted a poster on the wall proclaiming the dangers of

Aids and the need to place all bloodied items in the bin for incineration. Either people could not read the poster or there was very little awareness of how Aids was spreading. The state of this room had to be seen to be believed. Flies swarmed all around it and the only treatment on offer at this dental unit was extraction (without anaesthetic!). On a white tablecloth lay a row of different-sized pliers like something out of a chamber of horrors.

The doctors at the hospital were delightedly awaiting lorries from England, which were due to arrive with new beds, medicines and equipment. They came later that afternoon, two seven-and-a-half-ton trucks, one hired and one lent by Romford Post Office. Both trucks had driven the eighteen hundred miles from the UK across Europe, crossing the sea from Italy to Greece on the way. Previous convoys from the UK had not always had easy trips. A friend of mine had organized a convoy of lorries to Albania the previous year, and had been hijacked at gunpoint less than twenty miles outside the country. The trucks had been emptied of their cargo, which was valued at around £10,000. Albania was not as easy a destination to deliver aid to as Romania, and any who imagined it to be so faced a shock.

As the two trucks lined up in the centre of Korce, many people gathered to see these foreign vehicles, and a number of children started to peel off the GB sticker and unscrew the reflectors off the rear lights to keep as souvenirs. This was not an uncommon experience for drivers delivering aid, and they kept watch on their vehicles day and night. In Korce, a special underground storage room, an old bomb-proof bunker, was used as a warehouse for much of the aid to Albania, and the second lorry's cargo of optical equipment was put there.

Wedding and worship in Korce

That evening we had all been invited to the wedding of one of Redina's friends, which turned out to be quite an education. Both families had their own receptions prior to the wedding, and the whole of the bride's family gathered in the old school hall with a traditional Albanian band consisting of guitar, accordion and some makeshift instruments, which blared through a crackling old PA system and produced a distorted noise, while we all sat at a long table to eat about nine courses of Albanian food. There were vegetables and raw meat along with bottles of beer and rakki, a home brew which was a cross between whisky and gin. Throughout Albania, distilleries were set up on hillsides under plastic tents for the brewing of rakki, which is made with local herbs, a lot of sugar, and water from a nearby brook. It was a very potent brew indeed, about 150% proof; but the locals were knocking it back like orange juice. Just one sniff burnt a groove in the throat.

The bridegroom's family had had their pre-wedding reception the night before, at which the bride had made an appearance at around 11 o'clock. The groom and his family were to make a special entrance at the bride's reception. The fathers would shake hands and the mothers greet one another, and presents would be exchanged. This was all before the marriage ceremony took place. The couple would then go off to Tirana to be married in a civil wedding before returning to Korce for a joint wedding reception. This all proved to be quite an expense in this, one of the poorest European countries. Both fathers would be paying for it for a long time, unless they happened to be extremely wealthy, which very few were.

The next day it was good to be able to make our way to the local cinema, the venue for a newly formed church, which had been meeting for about eighteen months under the leadership of a Welshman, Mike Brown, of the Albanian Evangelical Trust. Around a hundred people gathered for the service, at which my fellow traveller, the Rev. David Beer, and I shared. The service lasted for about an hour and a half. About thirty members of the congregation were there probably for the first time, and a number of these made commitments. Most of the church's Bible study work was conducted during the week in homes. Redina was a leader in a women's study group, and many had come to know Christ as their personal Lord and Saviour through her.

In the afternoon, we wandered around the dusty streets of Korce, which were swarming with people out for their traditional Sunday walk. It was fascinating to see whole families – mum, dad, and perhaps six or ten children, all dressed in their Sunday best, walking arm in arm through the streets, greeting one another, relaxing, and enjoying their day off work. It was curious to see Sunday marked with such a display of family unity in a country where religious festivals of any kind had been banned, but such sights are common in Eastern European countries. All the shops were open, tempting Albanians with western products – washing machines, vacuum cleaners, irons, bicycles, Coca Cola, Mars bars, cigarettes, gloves, torches – all at prices above what the average Albanian family could afford.

While we were parading through the streets, we were taken into the house of a baker who had recently become a Christian, and there the family was busy stoking up the fires in the old-fashioned way, baking bread for the next day's sales. I chatted with the family about Jesus being the Bread of Life (John 6:35 and Matthew 4:4).

During our visit to Albania, Redina asked Mike and some of our party to help her with her baptism, which was to take place at Lake Ohrid, a vast and beautiful lake a few miles away from Korce. On the other side of the lake lay Kosovo, home to three million Albanians, as many as lived in Albania itself. Eighty per cent of Kosovo's residents were Albanian, but they suffered greatly under the Serbian authorities, who treated them as unwelcome refugees. Serbian soldiers often amused themselves by firing tear gas into their schools and playgrounds for the pleasure of seeing the children suffer. It was hard to believe that a world as cruel as that lay just over the hills.

A few friends and family members, some of whom were yet to become Christians, gathered on the lake's shore to hear Redina give her testimony and affirm her allegiance to Jesus Christ before walking out into the shallow water to be baptized by full immersion, while we sang choruses. It was one of the most memorable individual baptisms that I have ever attended. It was followed by a scrumptious picnic in a nearby park.

Sheep's eyes and raw meat

The next day we were to be met and taken somewhere at nine o'clock – give or take a couple of hours, as was my usual experience in Eastern Europe. So as not to waste the time, I started to distribute tracts in the street. People were keen to snatch them from my hands, and stopped immediately to read the free literature that had been given to them in their own language.

A number of them stopped, pointed up to God and crossed themselves. Many were Muslims, Catholics, or uncertain as to what Christianity was all about. Within the space of about two hours I had distributed something like two thousand tracts, as well as witnessing a fight which broke out because a man driving a van had bumped into someone else's car, bringing all the traffic to a standstill in this central part of town, while they argued it out with true Latin passion. In a land where insurance is non-existent, insurance details cannot simply be exchanged and a claim put in to the insurance company. The matter has to be argued out there and then in the hope of getting the best deal and a decent amount of money handed over to pay for the necessary repairs.

Eventually, Redina and her uncle arrived and we headed for some mountain villages. We drove about fifteen miles outside of Korce, off the main asphalted road and on to a dirt track, where we followed a young shepherd boy and his flock of sheep and goats. We then drove up a dry river bed into the dusty mountains and the area known in Bible times as Illyricum, then a Roman province stretching from Italy to Macedonia along the Adriatic.

Very poor villages could be found up in the mountains, where farmers used caterpillar tractors to plough the dark, stony land in the hope that any seed planted would bear a harvest. When we arrived at a small, medieval-style village of about thirty houses, the villagers gathered around our white Land Rover and stared at us intently. I noticed that none of the women and children wore shoes. Their feet were black with dirt, and cut and bruised. Most of the men who worked the land wore boots of some sort, and to have them was considered something of a status symbol.

A local farmer, who had recently become a Christian, showed us around his fields. We saw rakki being distilled in the village and a number of farmers sleeping off a draught or two. Chickens and cockerels roamed freely among open sewage. We were invited to inspect the sheep and cattle before being led into the farmer's home as honoured guests. We sat round a large table with the elders of the village, the equivalent perhaps of a British parish council, and listened to the rugged, ruddy, and stubble-faced men telling us about their hard life, their smiles showing their black and missing teeth. Women brought in food, including local delicacies, such as sheep's eyes, washed grapes, milk and raw meat with bread, and we all had to have a special tot of freshly-brewed rakki as a welcome to the village. Although none of us wanted to taste anything, it would have been impolite to refuse. I could not bring myself to eat the sheep's eyes, but I enjoyed the grapes, goat's milk and sheep's cheese, along with a minute sip of rakki.

While the rest of the team were saying farewell to the Christian family, I managed to take a look at one or two of the village homes, which were extremely bare. The floors were dusty, flies swarmed everywhere and water was provided by a simple well in the garden. It was unbelievable that people could live in such poor conditions.

Families were usually made up of three or four generations living under one roof, an arrangement which meant that older people were generally well cared for and respected by the younger members of their families.

Muslim hospitality

The next morning we awoke to the crisp, cool air of a late September day and I decided to take a walk around the streets of Korce, which had obviously seen better days. Everything was in poor repair, a shadow of its former glory. There were grand villas with balconies and wooden shuttered windows with vineyards behind walls and iron bars, obviously the former residences of quite wealthy Albanians. Many cities were badly affected by the devastating earthquakes of 1931 and 1960, which toppled minarets and flattened churches as well as thousands of homes.

I turned a corner and bumped into a Muslim family, who spoke no English but who bade me come into their home. I hesitantly accepted their invitation and went into the house, where I met grandparents, parents and ten children. They proudly showed me their television set with its new satellite dish and decoder, which enabled them to watch Disney cartoons on Euro satellite channels. They also showed off their ghetto-blaster. To have a television and a ghetto-blaster in such a poor country seemed to be the height of luxury and of material well-being. I was offered some Turkish coffee in a very tiny cup. The family were extremely friendly and I tried to communicate with them through sign language that I was a preacher and had come to tell people about Jesus. I was able to share a gospel tract with them before taking a picture of myself with them (at their insistence), which I later sent to them from the UK, as promised.

As I left them and walked on down the cobbled streets, I came across a large, open expanse of ground where shepherds were grazing their sheep. Other men were changing the sump oil on a Transit van, and some women were baking large flat pancakes and laying out bread mixture on blankets as others lit bonfires. This patch of land was obviously very useful to the local community.

Later that day we loaded our bags into the Land Rover and said goodbye to Korce, a town which now held many memories for me. As we returned along the narrow and winding road that had brought us there, I was glad that it had been dark on the way and that I had not then seen the sheer drop down the side of the hairpin roads which meandered up and over the top of the long mountain range.

As we descended one of the mountain ranges, we could see a small orange car heading up the road and a battered old coach coming down. It did not take much imagination to see that if the bus swung around the hairpin, taking up all of the road as it had been doing all the way down, and happened to time it badly, it would crash into this orange car, which was crawling up in first gear. The inevitable happened. The coach swung round a corner and smashed straight into the front of the orange car, pushing it back to within six feet of a sheer precipice which fell well over five hundred feet into the valley below.

The usual chaotic scene ensued: arm-waving bus driver, arm-waving occupants of the orange car. As we watched, David Beer, who is religious adviser to Anglia Television, kept the video camera rolling, got out of the Land Rover and went up close to the men who were arguing. One of the men pulled out a revolver and pointed it in David's direction until David took the hint and stopped filming. It was best not to hang around in this lawless country, where one could easily be shot before questions were asked.

After several more hours travelling, we stopped for a picnic at the side of a mountain road, a spot which reflected the beauty of this little-known Adriatic land, which, with much investment and a stable political situation, could become a real tourist attraction. It is a country that has everything: mountains, valleys, and stunning beaches and coastline.

Tirana: flies and faith

We arrived in Tirana in the rain to meet the Minister of Health, a Christian man in his early thirties, who was overseeing our aid distribution. Unfortunately, Albanian red tape meant that each item of optical equipment had to be recorded. There were forty thousand lenses, each needing to be itemized before any could be used, a task which would take about six weeks. This was bureaucracy gone mad in a country that was crying out for medical and optical equipment. The eighty-year-old optician who was travelling with us had planned to stay for several weeks to oversee the project, but out of sheer frustration he decided to return home with us.

While in Tirana we met a Baptist Missionary Society couple from Scotland, Drs Chris and Mairi Burnett, and their two boys. They were working for the European Baptist Federation, seconded from the BMS, assisting with a health programme in a local hospital and establishing Christian work throughout the capital. They were living with their small children in a four-roomed house split into two halves. One half was behind a secure iron gate and housed a kitchen/lounge area, off which was a small shower room. Across the courtyard, ten feet away, were Chris and Mairi's bedroom, which doubled as an office, and the boys' bedroom. I had never seen a house in two halves before, and understood from Mairi that when it rained or was extremely cold in winter, dashing from one part of the house to the other was not the most pleasant of experiences. Yet this was considered a sheer luxury in Albania, as most Albanians in the capital lived in tower blocks.

Mairi was concentrating her medical expertise on midwifery and was teaching English to a woman who was eight months pregnant. In return, this lady was teaching her Albanian.

David Beer and I spent a night with the Burnetts. Lying down to sleep on two settees, we watched a live lizard run up the inside of the wall, and swatted numerous mosquitoes, which were thriving in the hot humidity of a summer night.

The next day, Mairi showed us around the local market, which was a hive of activity. Peasants had come in from the surrounding country to sell their produce: vegetables, herbs, spices. The meat counter had to be seen to be believed – heads of cows, pigs, sheep, chickens, turkeys, rabbits, all crawling with flies. Cheese was being cut by the chunkload; people were smoking, coughing and handling the food without any gloves or regard for hygiene. It was fascinating to visit a 'hole in the wall' bakery, as it was known, where a family had converted their home into a bakery. There was a great queue of people lining up for their daily fresh bread, which came out of the hole in the wall piping hot. Although now (in 1992) there was sufficient food, only a year before, food had been in very short supply and rationing was the norm. In response to this, American aid had been flown in, and Chris and Mairi had discovered a shop where they could buy cans of American food.

For the rest of the day, David and I went exploring to observe daily life in this city where hundreds of people were walking or cycling along the potholed roads. We spotted a number of Mormons in their American suits, proselytizing and seeking converts. Jehovah's Witnesses and those offering the keys to Transcendental Meditation had also been reported, along with Hare Krishna – again, a situation current throughout Eastern Europe.

I had been given a message from the European Christian Mission to pass on to their main worker in this part of the world, Stephen Bell, who was living in Tirana. We finally found Stephen's home and managed to hear something of his work. He had been working in Kosovo's capital Pristina with Albanian students for about four years before Albania really opened up or missionaries were allowed to enter the country. He was due to be married later that year to a young Albanian woman. He shared news of the church in Tirana, which met in a puppet theatre in the centre of the city. It had been meeting for only eighteen months, but had grown from half a dozen to around 115 in that time. Two years previously, there had been no acknowledged Christian church whatsoever in Albania, and now there were at least twenty-two, a number which by 1995 rose to more than a hundred.

Also that afternoon, we met Youth With A Mission workers, who told us of the Albanian Encouragement Project, through which western Christian organizations were working to co-ordinate aid and evangelism, a project with which Chris Burnett was heavily involved and with great success. Some organizations had learnt from their earlier mistakes, when they had rushed into Romania and duplicated much of what other groups were doing. They had now realized that pooling their resources would be a much more efficient and effective way of promoting God's kingdom, and the AEP was the result of that recognition.

Concrete mushrooms

On our walk back from our visits, David and I noticed that there were hundreds of miniature air-raid bunkers dotted like mush-rooms in the streets throughout the city. It is reported that Enver Hoxha was ever fearful of an invasion from the West, so he stuck long spikes on poles throughout the countryside in the hope that western soldiers parachuting in would land on the spikes and be impaled before they touched Albanian soil. The bunkers, of which there were in excess of fifty thousand around the country, were to house Albanian soldiers and civilians so that they might assist in the defence of their nation should an invasion take place. Hoxha put out the lie that Albania was the richest nation in Europe and needed to be protected from poor and greedy westerners.

It was interesting to note how many young people there were in Tirana. It seemed that well in excess of 60% of the population were under the age of twenty-five. Many were studying at college and desperately learning the English language in the hope that it might be a passport to the West. Many young Albanians were trying to save as many American dollars as possible to buy a one-way passage out of Albania. Some had already left and were sending money back to their relations. Despite Hoxha's lies about western poverty, it was a common belief among Albanians that every westerner drove a Mercedes, wore a Rolex watch and a fur coat, ate caviar and drank champagne with every meal, and lived in palatial castles, as this was the kind of lifestyle they had viewed in western films and advertisements on television. Sadly, very few

Albanians were able to leave Albania to discover the truth for themselves.

As part of our tour of Tirana that afternoon, David and I took in the empty plinth where Hoxha's statue had once stood, and looked at the massive mural, painted above the Albanian museum, depicting victorious workers and soldiers beating Turks, who had once invaded the land. We visited the main hotel in the middle of town, which, despite being very dark and dingy because of the shortage of light bulbs, was still the best hotel in Albania.

Tirana's central mosque broadcast its call to worship while we were walking around, to which only faithful Muslims would have responded. In the future, I think it likely that with the support and encouragement of Muslims in other countries, Albania's Muslim population will seek to become more dedicated and possibly pose a threat to Christianity in that country.

We spent another evening with the Burnetts, which gave us, full-time Baptist ministers in Britain, an insight into the lives of missionaries, the sacrifices they make by living in a foreign land, and the pressures this brings to bear on their family life. They can often feel extremely isolated, vulnerable and unsupported. Unless they are very strong spiritually, disappointment and depression can easily set in.

The next morning, David and I interviewed Redina for a place at Spurgeon's College, and a year later she began a degree course in theology there. She went on to gain a Master's degree in theology before going to Oxford University to study for a PhD. She will no doubt be a great theological mind for the future church of Albania and a tower of strength for its work among women.

After this, our team left Albania, a country which we had come to love during our week-long visit. At the airport, a customs official demanded US $200 before we were allowed to leave. Stan waved our letter from the Minister of Health before his face in protest. We could not understand how those who had welcomed us with open arms a week ago were now charging us to leave their country. We eventually got through customs, however, and took off.

On arriving home, it took a while to acclimatize to the luxuries of English life after the poverty we had witnessed in Albania.

9

MISSION ALBANIA

Our own missionary trip to Albania was only one in a long history of such journeys. Christianity in that country claims apostolic foundation. We read in Paul's letter to the Romans that he preached the gospel throughout Philippi and Macedonia and travelled on the Via Egnatia on his way to Thessalonica, then the largest city on that great highway. It was from Thessalonica that the gospel spread throughout the region then known as Illyricum (now including part of Albania) and also Athens and Corinth. Paul travelled that road on his third missionary journey in around AD 59. He later wrote to the church at Rome: 'From Jerusalem all the way around to Illyricum, I have fully proclaimed the gospel of Christ' (Romans 15:19).

Paul may also have visited southern Albania. Writing to Titus after release from imprisonment in Rome, Paul charged him: 'Do your best to come to me at Nicopolis, because I have decided to winter there' (Titus 3:12). Nicopolis, which was a well-known winter resort just south of Corfu, was one of the major cities in Epirus, and was connected to the Via Egnatia and Durres by a branch highway through Butrint. Titus also visited Albania, as we read in 2 Timothy 4:10. He went to Dalmatia, a name synonymous with Illyricum and derived from the name of a local Illyrian tribe. Roman persecution of Christians in Illyricum began early. The first martyrs, Florin and Laurin of Ulpiana (near Pristina), were put to death during the reign of Hadrian (AD 76–138). Thus began a long history of suffering for the sake of the gospel in that region.

In the seventh century in the south of Armenia we find companies of people separate from the rest of the church, who seem to have been determined to preserve scriptural simplicity in worship and practice, and protest against what they saw as the corruption of their fellow believers. Our knowledge of their teaching and practice is vague, and much of the evidence about them comes from their enemies, who accused them of Manichaeism and Gnosticism. But even their enemies had to give testimony to the morality of their lives, and we know of their unflinching courage in the face of persecution. They were known as Paulicians. They spent much time reading the Scriptures and praying, and were against the cult of the Virgin and the saints and the use of images in worship. By the tenth century they had settled in Macedonia and Albania, and they spread rapidly among the Slavs, where they became known as the Bogomils, which means 'friends of God'.

In 1222, the Pope ordered the king of Hungary to invade the country, and a long period of war and devastation began. In 1291, the Inquisition was established in Bosnia and the Bogomil churches began to decline. By the time of the Reformation in the sixteenth century, Albania was in the hands of the Turks, and its Roman and Greek churches remained completely untouched by the Reformation taking place throughout the rest of Europe.

The Bible in Albanian

In 1817, the British and Foreign Bible Society printed a letter from the Rev. R. Pinkerton, in which he wrote: 'The furnishing of the Albanians with a New Testament at least in their own language is an object highly worthy of the attention of the British and Foreign Bible Society. They still have no part of the Word of God in their own tongue. Or should a Bible Society be established in one of the Ionian islands, giving to the Albanians a New Testament in their own tongue would certainly become an object worthy of its earliest and most zealous efforts.'

On 25 October 1819, he wrote: 'A translation of the New Testament into the Albanian language has entwined itself about my heart for these several years past, in such a way that I literally could not get rid of it. We must lose no time in getting it undertaken for the sake of the numerous lives of the Albanians who have spread themselves far and wide in the ancient countries of Illyricum, Epirus, Macedonia and Greece.' That same year, the Bible Society made a grant of £300 for the translation, printing and distribution of Scripture portions in Albanian, and Pinkerton lost no time in finding Evangelos Mexicos, a man well known to the Greek patriarchs of Constantinople, who had promised to assist in producing an Albanian New Testament. Two years later, in 1821, the translation was finished; and later that year the Rev. H. D. Leevres of the Bible Society had commissioned the translation of the Old Testament into Albanian.

After various revisions, the Albanian New Testament was printed in Corfu in January 1825. By the end of the next year it had been distributed and received with the greatest joy. In the 1830s a commission was undertaken to translate the Psalms into Albanian. In the 1850s, a fresh edition of the Albanian New Testament was printed, and in 1861 the Rev. Alexander Thomson was chosen to carry out the Bible Society's work in the Mediterranean region. He had worked in Constantinople for seventeen years as a Free Church of Scotland missionary to the Jews, and during that time had had ample opportunity to become intimately acquainted with the Society's operations. In 1863 he travelled throughout Albania to ascertain for himself the spiritual condition and needs of the nation. He reported with sadness a complete lack of missionary activity.

Resistance to the Bible

Between 1865 and 1883, a colportage programme was established by two men, Riedel and Davidson. They faced much opposition from the Turks, and from the Catholic, Orthodox, Roman and Greek Churches (as well as succumbing to long periods of ill health). In 1867 they visited Gjirokaster, and the following year Korce, Berat and Konica, where they sold two hundred copies of the New Testament. By the late 1860s they had sold over eight hundred Bibles between them.

In 1867, Constantin Christoforides, a son of a silversmith from Elbasan in Albania, and an excellent Greek scholar, produced a revision of the 1828 New Testament and, by the 1880s, of various Old Testament books as well. He became a colporteur and travelled throughout Albania, selling and promoting the study of the Scriptures in the Albanian language. In 1872, he distributed over a thousand copies, a measure of his reception from his fellow countrymen. Two further colleagues, Fischer and Polio, continued the work of spreading the gospel throughout the nation in the years that followed.

In 1883, resistance to the spread of the gospel led to the arrest of one colporteur, Sevastides, who was expelled and made to walk on foot over flooded country behind a mounted policeman, lodging at various prisons. After thirteen days he returned home to Barat, where he was released. He was utterly exhausted and was confined to bed for some weeks. He was a bold witness for the truth, testifying to Muslims and meeting denunciations from bishops by reading the Scriptures to people in cafés so that they might hear the truth for themselves.

In 1887, another colporteur, Michael, was beaten unconscious in Janina and his New Testaments burnt on the spot.

The work of colporteuring in Albania was overseen for the British and Foreign Bible Society by Gerasim Qirias, who was based in Korce, where he held meetings for the reading of Scripture and for prayer. Sadly, the strain of Qirias's work caused the death of his young wife in 1891, and, three years later, his own death at the age of thirty-five. The following year Christoforides died, and in 1899 Thomson died too. These men and their families had served the Albanian evangelical mission for the best part of a century, despite much hardship, pain and suffering, which led even to death for some.

Albania is by far the poorest nation in Europe, and yet, as we have seen, it has a rich Christian history going right back to the apostle Paul. The opposition that the gospel has faced in this nation, both past and present, has been enormous, yet its light has never been extinguished. The dedication and faithfulness of God's people in Albania are indeed a challenge to us all today, particularly in the

West, where the demands on Christians are not so great. As the West gives of its wealth and abundant experience, we must also be willing and gracious enough to receive lessons in spiritual fervour, commitment, humility and insight from our long-suffering brothers and sisters in Christ. We have much to learn from one another.

Some facts and figures: Albania today

Population

Total 3,521,000

Albanian	93.5%
Gypsy	2.5%
Greek	2.4%
Others	1.6%

Population of Tirana 238,000

	Congregations	Members	Affiliated
Evangelical groups	17	500	750
Pentecostal	12	350	583
Brethren	6	360	550
Roman Catholic	200	90,000	150,000
Albanian Orthodox	200	144,000	240,000
Jehovah's Witnesses	5	250	417

Non-religious make-up 41.9%
Muslims including Sunni and Bektashi 40%
Orthodox 10.9%

Ultimately, the successes of Mormons and Ba'hai could adversely affect evangelicals. Evangelical Christian input has been swift and the effects dramatic. Within eighteen months of the fall of Communism, sixteen mission agencies had entered the country for aid projects, evangelism and church-planting. By October 1992, there were over a thousand believers gathering regularly to worship the Lord in nineteen congregations and seventeen home groups. There is an evangelical witness in twenty-two of the thirty-two districts of the country. Working for the Albanian Evangelical Mission are fifteen missionaries, twelve with YWAM, eleven with Frontiers, ten with Operation Mobilisation, seven with Ancient World Outreach, six with the Brethren and three with International Teams.

Nearly half of all Albanians live outside Albania: 1.8 million in Kosovo, 700,000 in Macedonia, 32,000 in Montenegro, 320,000 in Italy and 12,000 in Greece. The Bible in standard Albanian was completed only in 1992.

(Source: *Conscience and Captivity* by Janice Broun)

The coastline of Albania is about two hundred miles long. It is only fifty miles across the Adriatic from Italy. No railway linked Albania to the outside world until 1986.

Abortion was banned in Albania, and consequently the birth rate is four times the European average. The population of Albania is expected to reach four million by the year 2000. The average age today in Albania is fifteen.

In 1988, Albania was represented at the first Balkan conference together with Yugoslavia (the host country), Romania, Bulgaria, Greece and Turkey. This was a most significant step.

Albanian update

In the first week of March 1997, the possibility of a civil war in Albania raised its ugly head. Over the previous two years, many Albanians had invested their savings in a pyramid-style investment programme. This had been supported by the government, which encouraged all Albanian citizens to use the scheme. The benefits and rewards were said to be enormous. An investment of 70,000 lek (about £410) was supposed to double in the space of three months. Many sold their homes and possessions to make the most of this opportunity. Serious concern was raised by the World Bank and the International Monetary Fund, but this was ignored in Albania.

The inevitable happened. The scheme went bankrupt, leaving hundreds of thousands of Albanians literally penniless overnight.

It has been suggested that the scheme was organized by an elaborate Mafia-style outfit like those of Romania and Russia, where the bubble had also burst. Those running the schemes had disappeared into the night air, extremely rich.

Albania's President, Sali Berish, was fighting to maintain order in central Tirana on Saturday 15 March, as many villages on the city outskirts succumbed to outright panic. Eleven people were killed and about a hundred and fifty reported injured. Controlled gangs, having raided army bases for weapons, looted cities and government premises. Friends of mine serving in Albania with the Baptist Missionary Society were trapped in the midst of this chaos. Fortunately, the wife and children were able to fly out before the trouble became too serious, but the husband was taken with other missionaries to the port of Durres, in the hope that Italian soldiers would get them to Italy. They arrived at midnight, and were met by scenes of total chaos as boats arrived to evacuate them and crowds of Albanians stormed the port. Bullets were fired, and sadly some Albanians were killed. The boats left without the missionaries, who spent seven cold hours on the concrete quayside; hundreds of Albanians gathered around them, hoping also for a passage to the West. Eventually, the missionaries were able to leave, but conditions remained unstable in Albania for months. The future looks extremely fragile and unstable.

Since the evacuation of the western missionaries, it has been revealed that new Albanian Christians have begun to organize themselves, leading churches, preaching and taking Bible studies. This is a step in the right direction, as local people begin to take on responsibility for the Christian life in their nation.

The savagery of the repression of all real and imagined opposition to the dictator Hoxha had been such that seven hundred thousand had been killed or imprisoned for long periods. A high proportion of the population had been coerced into spying on neighbours. The present democratic government faces an immense task in redressing the injustice of the past, constructing a modern viable state from virtually nothing, initiating a fair programme of land reform and giving hope to a demoralized people.

Muslims from the Middle East have mounted a massive effort to re-Islamize the country by means of missionaries, scholarships, aid, and the building of mosques. Catholics in the north and Orthodox in the south are reasserting their presence where they were once strong, and all three are pressing for stringent legislation to keep out other religions considered un-Albanian.

10

RUSSIA, 1993
McDonald's and the Mafia

Nine years after Ruth and I had delivered Bibles to Russia for Open Doors, Russian students at Spurgeon's College invited a team to lead a mission in conjunction with their home churches. For six months prior to the trip, we prepared ourselves, learning Russian songs and praying together.

At the time of our first trip, there had been just one main central Baptist church in Moscow. It then had over a thousand members. It had managed to plant over thirty churches around the vast Moscow area, and it was among these churches that our students would preach, teach and help with outreach.

On arrival at the Central Baptist Church we were divided into twos and introduced to our hosts. All of this was arranged by a former Spurgeon's student, Vladimir. Five of us were taken to the outskirts of Moscow, a drive of about an hour through a city filled with high-rise blocks. There was a great deal of congestion, as the Metro was being extended to the outer limit of Moscow, which was expanding by the month as new buildings were constructed. This created open sewers, which were an ideal breeding-ground for mosquitoes.

We had a lovely meal with our pastor for the week, Sergei Rebov, an assistant pastor at the Central Baptist Church, with oversight for some other churches. He was married with six children, and they all lived in an eighth-storey apartment which consisted of one bedroom, a lounge, a bathroom and a small box room. It was hard to imagine living in such conditions, and easy to understand why the family was now enjoying its summer holidays at its dacha in the country with the children's grandparents. One of the reasons for staying there in the summer weeks was that it was cheaper to live off the produce the family grew there, as well as being fun to swim in the nearby lakes.

Church growth

The day after our arrival, we were shown around Moscow and spent two hours at the space park, where we saw replicas of Sputniks, recalling that Russia was the first nation to put a man in space (Yuri Gagarin). This massive park stretches about three miles square, with buildings and fountains, museums, fun-fairs and places to buy food. We walked until we could walk no more, an experience which gave us an understanding of how vast this city of nine million people is, with its big parks, wonderful buildings and its beautiful river meandering through the heart of the city. As one enters the capital of the world's largest country, itself the world's sixth largest city and the command post of half of the twentieth century's world order, it is clear that it is, however, a poor relation to Russia's other great city, St Petersburg.

That evening it was back to the Central Baptist Church to preach. In addition to Sundays, services were held on Wednesdays and Fridays. Since the fall of Communism, the Sunday school had grown to five hundred children, with a further five hundred on the waiting-list. A building was under construction adjacent to the church just to house the Sunday school, and the church itself had grown to fifteen hundred members. As we gathered for the evening service on the Saturday, we noticed that two thirds of the congregation were women, who had been in church praying for at least two hours before the two-and-a-half-hour service commenced. It was a great joy to be able to bring a greeting and to share a message.

The next morning we were in the church again for the Sunday service, where we prayed beforehand with the twenty or so deacons and five ministers. The church was filled to overflowing. We were welcomed into the pulpit, from where we saw that every man was smartly attired in jacket and tie. It was again a great joy to be able to preach from the pulpit where Billy Graham and Luís Palau had preached a few years before.

Before we preached, a number of representatives from an American church stood up to share a message. Much to the dismay of the pastors and the congregation, they gave their greeting briefly and left, making their way through the crowded church, saying that they had several other churches to visit that morning before flying back to the US.

After the evening service, we attended the ensuing youth service in the attic of the building, and were well received by the young people.

Back at Sergei's flat, we ate supper at around midnight. Sergei was doing a tremendous job looking after his two guests without the help of his family.

The next day, after seeing such sights as Red Square, Lenin's tomb and the Kremlin, we met up with the rest of our team, except for two who were outside of Moscow. We heard that they were having a good time preaching in village churches. It was amazing to be able to walk around Red Square handing out tracts and preaching the gospel to Russians and tourists. Everyone who received a tract stopped and read it there and then. Those who understood English asked us many questions about Christianity, the church and life in the West. We had many good conversations. Individuals who showed a genuine interest in Christianity were given the address of the local Baptist church, where they could learn more and receive pastoral care. Our desire was not to distribute Christian tracts in a hit-and-run fashion, but to introduce many Muscovites to the truth of Christianity and to see them built into a growing, caring, local church. In so doing we were assisting local Baptist churches in their outreach programme in the capital.

We lunched at McDonald's, where the queue to get in went all the way down the street. There are now several McDonald's restaurants dotted around Moscow.

All over Moscow, it was easy to spot the Mafia in their limousines with darkened windows, Porsches and Mercedes, as they cruised round the city complete with mobile phones and, no doubt, guns under their jackets. We were conscious of news reports of the number of diplomats who had been killed by the Mafia. Others, not prepared to pay protection money, had also been 'wasted' by these merciless men.

An Orthodox monastery and a toy factory

The next day we visited Zagorsk. Zagorsk is the rather unpoetic Soviet name for the town around the Trinity Monastery of St Sergius, Russia's foremost religious and historical landmark, and a place of both spiritual and national pilgrimage. The monastery was founded in about 1340 by a monk, Sergius of Radonezh, now patron saint of Russia. He wielded enough moral authority to unite the country against the ruling Mongol Tartars, blessing the army of Dmitry Donskoy before it defeated the Tartars in 1380. As a 'lavra', an exalted monastery, and the main link in a chain of fort-monasteries defending Moscow, it grew enormously wealthy on gifts from tsars, nobles and merchants looking for divine support. Closed by the Bolsheviks, it was reincarnated after the Second World War as the Zagorsk Museum of History and Art. Now restored as a monastery, it houses approximately a hundred monks, an Orthodox seminary and one of the former Soviet Union's two church academies. It was the residence of the Patriarch and the administrative centre of the Russian Orthodox Church until 1988, when they were moved to Moscow.

In 1991, the Russian Orthodox Church had an estimated fifty million members, nearly all of them Russians, Belarussians and Ukrainians. Numbers are growing, thanks not only to the fall of Communism, but also to the spurt of nationalism which followed it, for the church is an innate part of many Russians' notion of what it means to be Russian. Between 1988 and 1990, the number of working churches grew from under seven thousand to nearly ten thousand – a figure which still compares poorly, however, with 1917's statistic of fifty thousand working churches. Lenin, taking on board Marx's view that religion is 'the opium of the people', soon confiscated church property, brought members of the church to trial, and submitted them to deportation and execution. Stalin also attempted to purge Russia of the church until 1941, when he decided that it could be useful in raising morale and encouraging a sense of patriotism in the fight against Nazi Germany. Khrushchev returned to the attack in the 1950s, closing about fifteen hundred churches and turning some of them into museums of atheism. It was not until the 1980s, when Mikhail Gorbachev was in power, that the situation for the church began to improve under the President's programme of liberalization.

In an Orthodox monastery, there is usually a special well where the water is supposedly holy. Zagorsk is no exception, and during our visit many Russians were gathering around this well and filling up jars and bottles with its water. They would take it to people who were sick and in need of help.

Zagorsk is also famous as a main centre for carved wooden toys, including the ubiquitous Matryoshka dolls: the outer doll can contain anything from six to fifty smaller dolls, depending on its size. On our way back we stopped at the toy factory. Our tour was a hilarious affair. The English-speaking guide gathered the sixteen of us, burly western students, in a circle as if we were school children, and told us a little story about bears, squirrels, foxes, ducks and swans, all of which could be found as wood carvings at the factory. To draw us into the story, she gave us all animal masks. One of our group had to dress up as a fairy, complete with wand.

Fallen idols

The next day we tried our hand at witnessing in a big park. The passers-by were very responsive to our singing and accepted our tracts. In one area of the park we noticed toppled monuments to Lenin, which had been dumped there in a sort of graveyard. These once great and giant statues had proudly adorned Moscow's parks and squares, but now lay forlorn and fallen in an obscure part of the city, where children and tourists clambered all over them, posing for family photographs.

An orgy of statue-toppling and renaming of streets and squares followed the collapse of Communism in the former Soviet Union and other eastern-bloc countries. Many statues of Lenin, once found in every town, were destroyed, while others were spirited away by entrepreneurs and found new homes in cities such as New York and Seattle.

An article in the *Sunday Telegraph* of 2 March 1997, headlined 'Where Lenin is still on his pedestal', reported that in the Black Sea port of Odessa in Ukraine, a solution had been found to deal with all the discarded statues of Lenin in that city. A memorial park has been established – a 500-yard alley in the Lenin Komsomol Park, lined with statues and busts of Vladimir Ilyich Ulyanov, Lenin's birth name. I saw these first-hand when I visited Odessa in June 1996. Tim Gould, a political analyst for the European Union, who has lived in Ukraine since the early 1990s, said: 'Odessa has always considered itself different from the rest of the Soviet Union. It is a city of merchants and traders, so it is not surprising that they should be the first to realize the commercial worth of the end of Communism, by establishing this memorial park.'

Gorky Park

The following day, the team set out to evangelize in Moscow's super-efficient Metro. This underground railway system is nothing like any found in the West. Every station is beautifully decorated with murals on the ceiling, and is spotlessly clean, with no litter or graffiti anywhere to be found. Catching a train from one of these stations is like catching a train in the middle of the Sistine Chapel or some historic art gallery, something Moscow's commuters enjoy daily as they go about their business. Once again, our tracts were eagerly taken and immediately read by passengers.

This underground evangelism was a preamble to our open-air evangelism in Gorky Park. This park stretches almost three kilometres along the river upstream of the Krymsky Bridge. It is the city's official central park of culture and rest, and is named after the Soviet writer, Maxim Gorky. It features straight ornamental lakes where black swans cruise between pedal boats, a fun-fair with stages and auditoriums for further entertainment (which could be anything from rock concerts to lectures on science), and plenty of places to buy refreshments or flowers. It is popular with families as a place to spend a weekend afternoon.

About fifteen of us were present as we started singing songs in Russian and English and giving out tracts to passers-by, with whom we began to converse. Many of the young people we spoke to wanted to practise their English. We had a number of young Russian Christians in our party who were able to interpret for us, and we had many interesting conversations with soldiers, army officials and police as well as a number of tourists. As I watched our team, I reflected on the very different circumstances under which I had handed over Bibles nine years earlier. Prayers for freedom had been answered, and people were inquisitive and eager to know more about Christianity. There was no hindrance to the preaching of the gospel, although now there are those in Orthodox and government circles who would hinder the freedom of many non-Orthodox religious groups.

For example, at the time of our visit, a number of Swedish and American charismatic churches, which had been planted twelve months previously, were growing at a rapid rate and attracting congregations of between a thousand and fifteen hundred. Students from universities and colleges, in particular, were flocking to these churches, drawn by their modern forms of worship and charismatic style. The Russian Orthodox Church, which was losing young people from its congregations, was eager to have such foreign groups branded as cults and banned from hiring public buildings.

As we left Gorky Park through its magnificent gate towering sixty feet high, we sensed an air of unrest in the city streets around us. We noticed a man and a woman arguing as they drove by in a car. The car suddenly stopped, and the man got out and thumped his wife in the face. She screamed in pain. A number of our team went to help her, but the man jumped back in and drove off rapidly. We suspected that he was the worse for drink, which was a common problem in a city which, like many of its western counterparts, faces unemployment, drug abuse, and an increase in crime, prostitution and pornography.

Unrest and the Mafia

In the evening, most of us were involved in church activities, but the next day we were free to roam the Kremlin with all its chapels and attractions. It was wonderful to witness the beauty of these buildings, which were steeped in tsarist history and Russian Orthodox religion. At the heart of the Kremlin are some of the great Orthodox chapels, forbidden to visitors for decades. Further round on our sightseeing tour, we recognized the buildings we had seen on the television news in 1992, when Boris Yeltsin climbed aboard a tank in the overthrow of Communist rule and was hailed a hero by ordinary Russians. The building known as the White House, the Parliament building, was bombarded by tanks in a brief coup.

We sensed that Russians were still living through turbulent times and that further unrest was likely. Some older people wanted a return to Communist rule, under which food and work had been guaranteed. The market economy was giving way to an increase in greed, materialism and crime of a most vicious and degrading nature. We felt it a privilege, as students of theology, to be able to witness this significant period of Russia's history.

A week is probably needed to do the Kremlin justice and take in the treasures of the tsars. All around the site were money-changers ready to change roubles for dollars, a common sight in Moscow. Young children stood selling souvenirs such as post-cards, badges and old Russian military caps to foreign tourists. Buskers and beggars, some drunk, struggled on the sidelines to make ends meet in a society which had passed them by.

More joyous to witness were the newlyweds who passed by the eternal flame just outside the Kremlin's walls. It was traditional to come to the flame straight after the wedding in order for the marriage to be blessed with good luck. It was also considered a mark of respect to those who had lain down their lives in the century's two world wars.

We had the chance to go souvenir-hunting on the next day, our last. There are a number of shopping-malls close to Red Square where western products can be found alongside traditional Russian gifts. Such malls are also frequented by members of the Mafia, who exchange money and sell their own wares: cigarettes, wine, watches and perfumes. One of our group needed to exchange some more money, but did not trust the exchangers on the streets. He found a bank and asked the cashier for roubles to the value of US $50. She looked somewhat sheepish when she responded with the rate, adding that he would do better if he used the exchanger on the corner, a large man with the look of a Mafia godfather, smoking a cigar beside a table stacked with roubles.

Baptist links

Later, a number of us travelled to an orphanage on the edge of Moscow to observe something of the church's work with disabled children. One of the leading lights behind this social work was the Rev. Mikhail Zhidkov, a very sprightly pastor in his seventies, who helped in prisons and orphanages and with feeding many of the street children who wander around Moscow's train station.

Zhidkov was one in a line of Russians who had received training at Spurgeon's College. He came in the 1950s, and was followed in 1968 by Benjamin Fadischken and in 1969 by Walter Mitskevich. The first Russian to study at Spurgeon's was Robert Fetler, who trained there from 1912 to 1915. Fetler was a very influential pastor in St Petersburg until he was recalled to the Russian army in 1916. It is believed that he died in 1940 or 1941 after suffering torture and imprisonment for his faith.

The Baptist Church in northern Russia owed its origin to a visit by Lord Radstock, a British Baptist. While in France, he met a Russian princess, Madame Chertkova, the wife of the General Adjutant to the Tsar. She was so impressed by his preaching that she invited him to St Petersburg to preach among her family and friends. He first visited the then Russian capital in 1874, and preached in the houses and palaces of the Russian aristocracy. His work bore much fruit, and he witnessed the conversion of counts and colonels, who in turn shared their new-found faith with the peasants on their estates, and began to print and distribute tracts and initiate philanthropic projects. This new group of Christians became known as 'Pashkovites' (after one Colonel Pashkov), though some referred to them as Radstockites.

After our visit to the orphanage, we preached again in our churches and then bade farewell to our Russian friends. The next day we gathered at the Central Baptist Church to leave, only to discover that the coach Vladimir had booked for us had not arrived. On making enquiries, we discovered that the booking had been registered and payment received, but that more was demanded before the coach could be sent. This seemed to be regarded as a legitimate way of doing business in the new Russia as it took on board the values of a market economy. We ended up squeezing into a number of cars, and made it to the airport with just enough time to say farewell to my host, Sergei, who had been a great help during our visit. Some of the students would have liked more opportunity to evangelize and less to see the sights, but they agreed that it had been the trip of a lifetime, in which they had enjoyed Russian hospitality, witnessed a country in change and learnt something of what God was doing in the great nation of Russia.

Some facts and figures: Russia today

Of Russia's population of 153,646,000 (1995), 55% are reported to be Orthodox, 8.7% Muslim, 0.7% Protestant, 0.6% Buddhist, 0.5% Catholic and 0.4% Jewish.

Muslims, who number around fifty million (that is, one in every five former Soviet citizens), are the former USSR's fastest-growing religious group. Most are Turkic speakers from Central Asia, the Caucasus and the Middle and Lower Volga. The latter are mainly Tartars, descendants of Russia's medieval rulers. Others include the Persian-speaking Tadjiks. Nearly all are Sunni Muslims, except for the Shia Muslims of Azerbaijan and Dagestan, and some Ismailis.

Protestant congregations		Members	Affiliated
Eurasian Baptist	1,200	150,000	429,000
Lutheran		102,000	170,000
Pentecostal	400	35,000	130,000
Unregistered Pentecostal	250	30,000	107,000
Seventh Day Adventist	205	38,000	98,000
Baptist	80	10,000	20,000
Unregistered Baptist	125	10,000	20,000
Reformed Church		3,000	6,000

Russian update

During the course of 1997, a Bill passed repeatedly between Parliament and President Yeltsin, which would have restricted the activities of any religious group not officially registered before at least the last fifteen years. Such a law would have inhibited the movements of sects and cults such as the 'Moonies', the Jehovah's Witnesses, the Mormons and Hare Krishna, but Protestant churches were ranked as equally dangerous.

On 19 September 1997, however, the Russian Duma voted down a motion to delay the religious Bill by 357 to six. It has no power to initiate an attempt to override Yeltsin's veto of the July religious Bill. Sadly, however, this vote means that the passage by the Federal Council is now certain to bring into law the religious restrictions that had been feared. Only time will tell what effect this will have upon the churches of Russia in years to come.

11

BULGARIA AND
MACEDONIA, 1994
No end of problems

I paid a second visit to Sofia in the first week of January 1994, to meet Theodore Anglov and Spurgeon's College student, Evgeniy, who was home for the Christmas holidays and spending time with his fiancée and family.

It was a very cold, snowy day, about –3°C, and the traffic in Sofia was heavily congested as we dodged trams and buses to get to our restaurant for lunch, where I had talks with Dr Anglov concerning ways in which the Evangelical Alliance Bulgaria Support Group could help the Christians in Bulgaria. He explained that inflation was a big problem in the country, and that many Bulgarians had been struggling to make ends meet, as they had done in the first winter after the fall of Communism. Much aid from the West had been shipped in at that time and distributed through church networks to children, the elderly and the needy. There had been frequent power cuts for lack of fuel, and the levels of crime, violence, prostitution, drug dealing, alcoholism and unemployment had all increased.

I learnt that opposition from the Orthodox Church was rising against non-Orthodox churches. No distinction was made between Mormons, 'Moonies', Jehovah's Witnesses, Transcendental Meditation groups and Protestant churches such as the Baptists, Methodists and Pentecostals. The Orthodox Church resented the growth of these churches as its own membership declined.

Young people in particular were leaving the state church, and Orthodox priests were trying to stem the exodus. Protestant Churches had no real voice in the media, and during Communist rule a rumour had circulated that Baptists ate babies for breakfast. Now it was rumoured that young people were drawn to the Free Churches because drugs were handed out at services, which were covers for orgies. I was told that these lies were broadcast on radio and television, and the only way Dr Anglov and his colleagues could counter them was to have special open evenings to which the young people's parents could come to have their minds put at rest and their questions answered.

On the positive side, the government had offered the Baptist Union the gift of a ten-acre plot of land on which to build a church, an orphanage and a Bible college. Fearing that the Orthodox-influenced Communists would want this land back once the project had been completed, the BU decided to pay for the land, despite the fact that it cost US $50,000, and to start to dig the foundations themselves. As expected, the authorities had demanded the land back, even though the sale had been completed. It was only after former US President, Jimmy Carter, had intervened, that the BU won this long-running battle with the government and succeeded in having the land officially signed over to them.

Their struggle had been just one sign of continuing government opposition. The door which had opened when Communism fell was beginning to close rapidly. Communism had not completely disappeared from many of the countries where it had formerly held such a tight rein. Many Eastern Europeans complained that its perpetrators had merely paled from red to pink. Many of the same people were still in power and maintained a Communist way of thinking, trying to dictate, controlling by force, and preventing freedom of speech and of religion.

The day after my meeting with Dr Anglov, I travelled again to Skopje, this time on a rickety old bus. Within the first five minutes of my journey I discovered that the man sitting next to me was a Swedish Christian missionary in his twenties who was returning to work at a Pentecostal church in Skopje. We chatted together about Christianity in Eastern Europe and witnessed to a Bulgarian soldier and some young people travelling with us.

Orthodox Christmas

On arrival at our destination, the Swede invited me to meet some of his friends. As we walked through the town centre, we noticed that there was music, singing and dancing in the main square. It was around midnight, but thousands of people, parents and young children, filled the place. Children were singing and dancing on a stage; there was a firework display and a big Christmas tree; and people were carrying green-berried branches similar to mistletoe. We were amazed, and upon enquiry discovered that it was Christmas Eve in Macedonia – Orthodox Christmas Eve, which falls on 5 January.

We eventually made our way to my companion's accommodation, where his friends made us very welcome. The team I met was working among university students for a year. Each member was sponsored by a Swedish church, and the commitment and dedication of all involved were greatly to be admired.

I was later collected by the friend I had come to visit, Bore, in whose house I awoke the next morning to a beautiful Christmas Day. We paid a visit that holiday to some members of the local Baptist church I had met on my previous trip to Skopje, and I handed over some money which had been given by the Baptist Missionary Society. Funds had flooded in to help with the distribution of aid to the many refugees in the Yugoslavian states of Bosnia, Croatia, Serbia and Kosova. On the day of my visit, the church was about to distribute the thirty parcels they gave out every month to thirty refugee families. It had also turned the basement of its building into accommodation for refugees.

The atmosphere in Skopje had changed since my last visit eighteen months previously. The threat of a Serb invasion had waned under the presence of United Nations forces. In the church, changes had taken place, too. The pastor I had met last time had decided to move to America, leaving the leadership to his brother, a chemical scientist, and disappointing the congregation, who were now without a theologically trained pastor.

Later in the morning I waited at the border with Kosova for a Pentecostal pastor to whom I had agreed to hand over some money for his church in Pristina and with whom I planned to discuss how best to help his congregation further. We waited three hours in the freezing cold for the queue of cars at the border to pass through, many of them no doubt transporting fuel to Serbia, where it could be sold for four times its price in Macedonia.

After spending the rest of Christmas Day with members of the Skopje church, I bade farewell to my Macedonian brothers and sisters and headed back to Sofia, where I called on Pastor Nikolay Nedelchev, Principal of the Bulgarian Bible Academy, Logos, who gave me encouraging reports of the daily growth of the academy.

Continuing connections

My continuing links with Bulgaria have been mainly through the Evangelical Alliance Bulgarian Support Group, which was established in 1992 as the result of a Bulgarian Day by the EA. This committee is made up of people from several Christian organizations (Scripture Union, Open Doors, Evangelical Missionary Alliance, Saltmine Trust, Operation Mobilisation, Youth With A Mission and some individuals), all of which have a desire to see the church in Bulgaria strengthened and encouraged. The group continues to raise finances to support theological students at the Bulgarian Baptist Union Seminary and the Logos Institute, as well as to raise awareness of the needs of Bulgaria in the West.

The Bulgarian students who trained at Spurgeon's College, Evgeniy Naydenov and Teddy and Diddy Oprenov, have now returned to their country and are putting into practice all that they learnt during their studies. Evgeniy is assistant pastor of the large Methodist church in Sofia and a teacher at Logos. Teddy and Diddy are working with the Central Baptist Church alongside Theodore Anglov, and teaching in the Baptist Theological School. I believe that their input and knowledge will be a great strength to the church in the months and years ahead. Other young Bulgarians have followed in their footsteps.

On Saturday 25 May 1996, the former king of Bulgaria, Simeon II, returned to his homeland after fifty years in exile. The fifty-eight-year-old monarch, exiled in childhood by the Communists, was met by the mayor of Sofia and members of the monarchist groups. Before his visit he had expressed surprise that the government had granted him permission to enter the country.

He was due to meet President Zhelev during his stay. Thousands of people lined the route from the airport as his motorcade arrived at Alexander Nevski Square. The crowd sang the old Bulgarian national anthem and chanted his name as cathedral bells rang out.

The winter period of 1996 was an extremely difficult time for all Bulgarians, thanks to the harsh weather and escalating inflation sweeping the nation. The Bulgarian Baptist Union established a winter relief fund to try to help the elderly and very young survive the terrible conditions. There was a shortage of bread across the nation, and aid was sent from the West to help alleviate the hardship endured by the Bulgarian people.

Some facts and figures: Bulgaria today

Population

Total 9,036,000

Slavs	84%
Bulgarian	6,950,000
Macedonian	225,000
Russian	18,000
Serb	9,000
Czech	9,000
Turks and Pomarks	11%
i.e. approx.	1,000,000
Gagauz	12,000
Crimean Tartar	6,000
Gypsy	4.6%

speaking Romany, Turkish or Bulgarian

Population of Sofia 1,222,000

Bulgaria is one of Europe's poorest countries. Communism bequeathed a legacy of pollution caused by inefficient industries. Since 1990, some progress is liberalizing the economy, which is adapting to market forces. Great poverty remains, but there is much potential for growth. Public debt is about US $1,220 per person.

	Congregations	Members	Affiliated
Assemblies of God	280	30,000	43,000
Church of God	140	15,000	25,000
Seventh Day Adventists	75	4,500	8,040
Brethren	150	4,500	7,500
Congregational	54	5,000	6,250
Methodist	17	1,700	4,250
Turkish independent groups	50	4,000	7,000
Baptist	30	2,000	3,000
Catholic	30	30,000	75,000
Bulgarian Orthodox	3,895	4,440,000	6,000
Armenian Orthodox	11	14,600	20,000

The Bulgarians' political and spiritual transformation has been one of the most dramatic in the former Communist bloc. The greatest change is among evangelicals, whose numbers have more than doubled in three years. In Sofia they have quadrupled. Evangelistic outreach among Bulgarians has had positive results among Turks and Gypsies, with thousands coming to Christ over the past six years. Amid this growth of evangelicalism, every modern heresy and cult seem to have targeted the country – Mormons, Children of God, Jehovah's Witnesses, extreme prosperity teaching, Transcendental Meditation, Hare Krishna and Ba'hai can all be seen selling their wares on the streets of Sofia. The Orthodox Church has strongly opposed these sects and has included evangelicals among them.
(Source: *Operation World*)

Bulgarian update

Throughout 1997, both Bulgarian and Macedonian evangelical churches have faced tremendous opposition from the Orthodox Church, and from the national governments, which it influences considerably. Strict laws have been passed in both countries in the hope of curtailing evangelical growth and development. The police have threatened Baptists in Macedonia with the closure of their church building unless they carry out work to meet stringent safety regulations (erecting a lightning conductor and installing a fire hydrant, more fire extinguishers, emergency lighting and telephones). The authorities know that the cumulative cost of such installation is far beyond the hundred or so Macedonian Baptists, who have appealed to western Baptists to assist them in their plight. In Bulgaria, too, times are hard for evangelical Christians as they battle against soaring inflation (600%) and harsh winters. In spite of this, evangelical churches continue to grow, and by 1997 the Baptists had grown to sixty-six congregations with over four thousand members.

Theodore Angelov, speaking at the Evangelical Alliance Bulgarian Consultation Day in Northampton in October 1997, said, 'Many would not turn to the church in better times, but because of the difficult situation throughout the country, caused by unemployment and inflation, now is the time to respond to the needs through the preaching of the gospel, in order that many may be added to the kingdom of God.'

CONCLUSION

As churches and Christians in the West, we have much to learn from our brothers and sisters in the East. Their decades of faithful service to the Lord, even in the face of fierce persecution and threats of death, are an example of bold Christianity. Although the Christian church in the East has suffered greatly in the past, their future looks bright. Since the collapse of Communism, and changes in the laws on religion, it is hoped that the church will grow from strength to strength. However, the church now has new enemies in the shape of materialism and secularism as well as pyramid savings plans, alcoholism, drug abuse, prostitution, child abuse, glue-sniffing, Mafia-controlled protection rackets, pornography, homelessness and a rapid increase in crime. All these things, as well as being severe problems in themselves, erode the opportunities Eastern European Christians now have to proclaim the gospel.

In many countries throughout Central and Eastern Europe, the Orthodox church seeks to impede evangelical growth and development. Because of the strong Orthodox influence, evangelicals are often denied access to the media, marginalized when they seek community involvement, and prevented from hiring public buildings for acts of worship. In some parts of Eastern Europe, the Orthodox church has taken extreme measures. Evangelical ministers have been beaten up, and their homes, churches and cars set on fire, by local communities who have been led to believe that evangelicals are enemies of both church and state. This quasi-religious nationalism is present at every level of society, from the school gate through to the college lecture room and on to the workplace.

Christian leadership and theologically trained ministers are essential if the church is to mature and grow in spiritual understanding, depth and numbers. Continued support from churches in the West through twinning programmes, prayer initiatives, accountable giving and social-action support projects are all still very much needed. The threat of growing cults and, indeed, the force of Islam will be a challenge not only to churches in the West, but increasingly to those in the East as well.

I hope that this book and the stories I have recounted will show something of how God has been moving over the past two decades to strengthen his church and to provide opportunities for evangelism such as have never been known before. There is a sense of optimism and of great opportunity as we move towards the new millennium.

If you feel that you, your family or your church could help to support God's work in Central and Eastern Europe, then please look at the resources section of this book or contact me at the address given there.

RESOURCES

Books and articles

Amnesty International, *Albania - Political Imprisonment and the Law* (1984)

Robin Blount, *European Church Partnership: A User's Guide to Church Twinning: Christianity and the Future of Europe* (Westcott House, 1994)

Janice Broun, *Conscience and Captivity: Religion in Eastern Europe* (Ethics and Public Policy Centre, Washington DC, 1988)

Bub Bultmann, *Revolution by Candlelight* (Multnomah, 1991)

Anita and Peter Deyneka, *Christians in the Shadow of the Kremlin* (Hodder and Stoughton, 1992)

David Edwards, *Christians in a New Europe* (Collins, 1990)

Darra Goldstein, *A Taste of Russia* (Sphere, 1987)

Hermann Hartfeld, *Faith Despite the KGB* (Pickering, 1980)

David Hathaway, *Checkmate* (Lakeland, 1974)

Ruth March, *Europe Reborn* (OM Publishing, 1992)

Samuel Nesdoly, *Among the Soviet Evangelicals* (Banner of Truth, 1986)

Jay Meridel Rawlings, *Gates of Brass* (International Vista, 1985)

Michael Rowe, *Russian Resurrection* (Marshall Pickering, 1994)

David Stanley, *Eastern Europe on a Shoestring* (Lonely Planet, 1989)

Laszlo Tokes, *With God for the People* (Hodder and Stoughton, 1990)

Joseph Ton, *Marxism, the Faded Dream* (Marshall Pickering, 1976)

Richard Wurmbrand, *If That were Christ, Would you Give him a Blanket?* (Hodder and Stoughton, 1970)

Religion, State and Society (journal of the Keston Institute) 24.3 (1996)

Agencies

The addresses listed are in the UK unless otherwise stated.

A = aid, C = childcare, E = evangelism, L = literature,
R = research

Albanian Evangelical Trust

PO Box 388
Wrexham
Clwyd
LL11 2TW

tel. 01978 354006
A E L

Assist Europe

Phil South
PO Box 789
Sutton Coldfield
West Midlands
B74 2XJ

tel. 0121 323 3701
fax 0192 344 2892
email 100537.367@compuserve.com
A

Baptist Missionary Society

PO Box 49
Baptist House
129 Broadway
Didcot
Oxfordshire
OX11 8XA

tel. 01235 512077
fax 01235 511265
email 100626.1577@compuserve.com
A E L

Baptist World Alliance

6733 Curran Street
McLean
Virginia 22101-6005
Washington
USA

tel. 703790 8980
email BWA@bwanet.org
A

Blythswood

Main Street
Lochcarron
Strathcarron
Ross-shire
IV54 8YD

tel. 01520 722337
fax 01520 722264
email 100423.1535@compuserve.com
A L

East European Literature Advisory Committee

Gerry Davey
3 Florence Road
Bromley
Kent
BR1 3NU

tel. 0181 464 0460
fax 0181 313 1373
email 100117.2360@compuserve.com
L

East European Ministries

Rev. Clive Doubleday
117 Kingsway
Petts Wood
Kent
BR5 1PP

tel./fax: 01689 603680
email CliveDoubleday@compuserve.com
A C E L R

Euro Evangelism/Euro Aid

Gary Cox,
PO Box 50
Kingswood
Bristol
BS15 1EX

tel. 0117 961 5161
fax 0117 935 2127
email 106020.3202@compuserve.com
A E L

European Christian Mission

50 Billingham Road
Northampton
NN1 5DR

tel. 01604 21092
fax 01604 20594
email 100344.2443@compuserve.com
A E L

Evangelical Alliance Bulgarian Support Group

Mrs Jenny Butlin
Beech House
London Road
Washington
Pulborough
West Sussex
RH20 4BA

tel./fax 01983 872573
email windlesham.pupils@rmplc.co.uk
A C E L R

Evangelical Missionary Alliance

Rev. Stanley Davies
Whitefield House
186 Kennington Park Road
London
SE11 4BT

tel. 0171 207 2156
fax 0171 207 2159
email sdavies@ema.co.uk
E

International Fellowship of Evangelical Students

(office for Europe and CIS)
Kennett House
108–110 London Road
Headington
Oxford
OX3 9AW

tel. 01865 308801
fax 01865 308802
email IFES@compuserve.com

Keston Institute

Canon Michael Bourdeaux
4 Park Town
Oxford
OX2 6SH

tel. 01865 311022
fax 01865 311280
email keston.institute@keston.org
R

Light in the East

Licht im Osten
Zuffenhauser-Str. 37
D-70825
Korntal-Munchingen
Germany

email lio@lio.org
E L

Love Russia

Love Russia House
28A Park Street
Bordon
Hampshire
GU35 0EB

tel./fax 01420 477668
email love.russia@ukonline.co.uk
A C L

International Media for Ministry (No Frontiers)

Mr and Mrs D. Milborrow
PO Box 11
Tunbridge Wells
Kent
TN2 3EY

tel. 01892 549141
fax 01892 529500
email nofrontiers@compuserve.com
L

Open Doors

PO Box 6
Witney
Oxfordshire
OX8 7SP

tel. 01865 300262
fax 01865 300706
email 106333.1732@compuserve.com
L

Operation Mobilisation

The Quinta
Weston
Rhyn
Oswestry
Shropshire
SY10 7LT

tel. 01691 773388
fax 01691 778378
email info@uk.om.org
A E L

Release International

Brian Loader
PO Box 19
Bromley
Kent
BR2 9TZ

tel. 0181 460 9319
fax 0181 290 4585
email release.international@aol.com
A E L

Romanian Aid Fund

2 Torquay Grove
Woodsmore
Stockport
SK2 7BB

tel. 0161 612 9013
fax 0161 612 9015
email RomAidFund@aol.com
A E L

Saltmine Trust

Peter Barnes
4 Linden Road
New Costessey
Norwich
Norfolk
NR5 0BE

tel./fax 01603 743786
email 113041.1117@compuserve.com

Samaritan's Purse International

Victoria House
Victoria Road
Buckhurst Hill
Essex
IG9 5EX

tel. 0181 559 2044
fax 0181 502 9062
email 100067.1226@compuserve.com

Scripture Union

International Relations Secretary
207/209 Queensway
Bletchley
Milton Keynes
MK2 2EB

tel. 01908 856000
fax 01908 856111
email scriptureunion.org.uk
E L

Slavic Gospel Association

Trevor Harris
37A The Goffs
Eastbourne
East Sussex
BN21 1HF

tel. 01323 725583
fax 01323 739724
email sga@JIREH.co.uk
L

Spurgeon's Child Care

74 Wellingborough Road
Rushden
Northamptonshire
NN10 9TY

tel. 01933 412412
fax 01933 412010
email SpurgeonsChildCare@compuserve.com
C

WEC International

Bulstrode
Gerrards Cross
Buckinghamshire
SL9 8SZ

tel. 01753 884631
fax 01753 882470
email 100546.1550@compuserve.com
E L

Youth With A Mission

The Oval
Ambrose Lane
Harpenden
Hertfordshire
AL5 4BX

tel. 01582 463300
fax 01582 463213
email 101317.2566@compuserve.com
A E L

For further details or correspondence with the author, write to:

The Rev. Clive Doubleday
117 Kingsway
Petts Wood
Kent
UK
BR5 1PP

tel./fax 01689 603680
email CliveDoubleday@compuserve.com

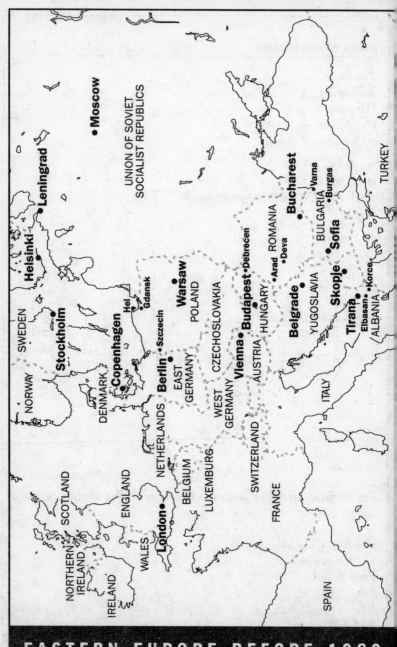

EASTERN EUROPE BEFORE 1989

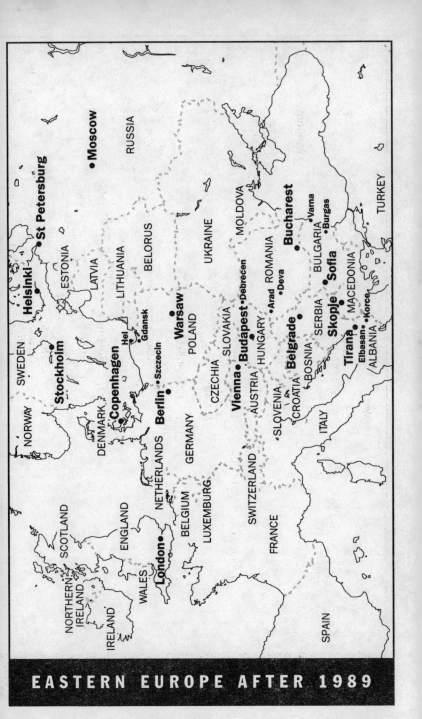

EASTERN EUROPE AFTER 1989